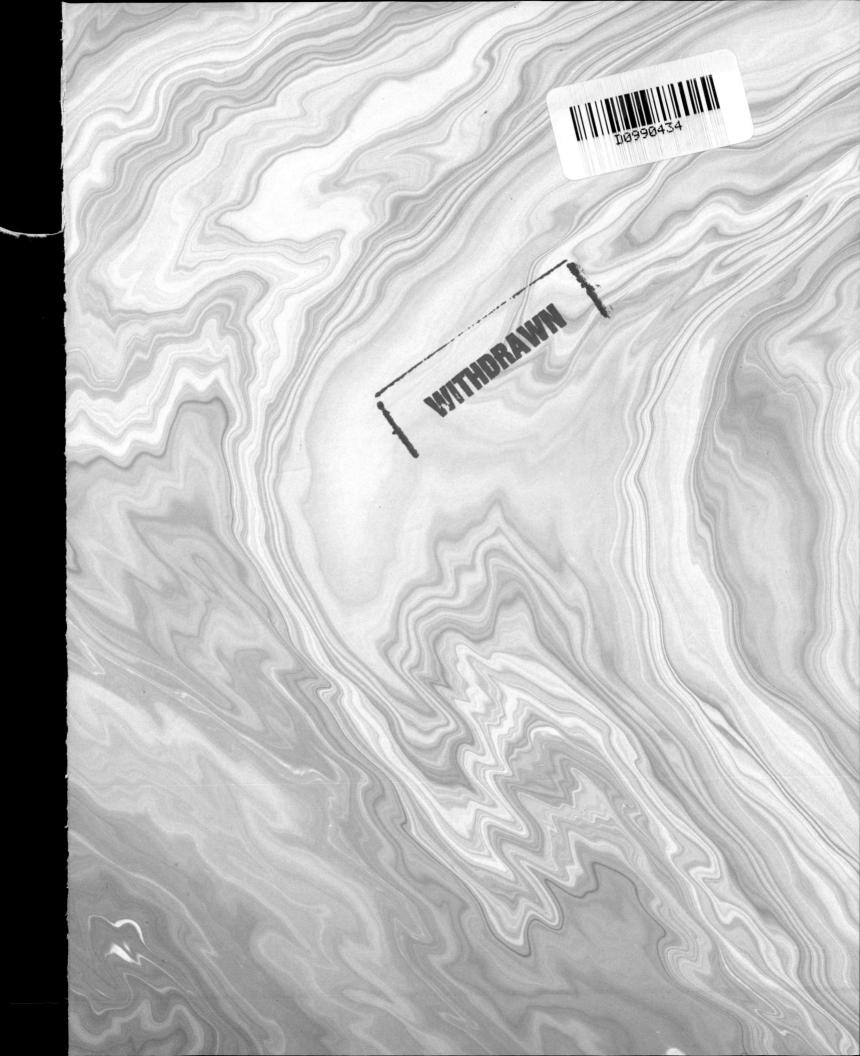

Hull Pottery

Decades of Design

Jeffrey B. Snyder

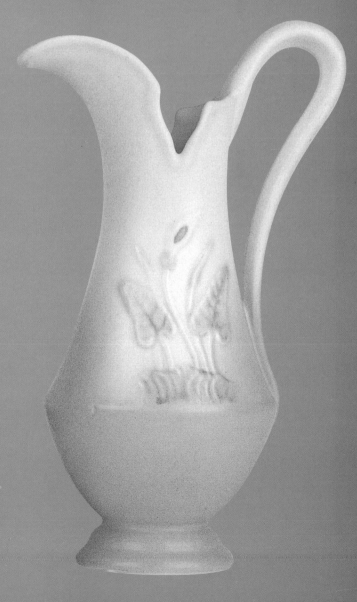

4880 Lower Valley Road, Atglen, PA 19310 USA

To Dick, Terri, Adam and Matt ...
fellow pumpkin patch explorers!

Values

The values found in the captions are in United States dollars. Values vary immensely based on the location of the market, the rarity of the items, and the enthusiasms of the collecting community at any given time. Values in the Midwest will surely differ from those in the West or East, and those at specialty shows or auctions will differ from those in dealers' shops.

All of these factors make it impossible to create absolutely accurate values listings, but a guide to realistic pricing may be offered. These values are not provided to set prices in the collectibles marketplace, but rather to give the reader a realistic idea of what one might expect to pay for Hull pottery in mint condition. I wish you luck in your quest for these exciting and dynamic wares.

—Jeffrey B. Snyder

Library of Congress Cataloging-in-Publication Data

Snyder, Jeffrey B.
Hull pottery: decades of design/Jeffrey B. Snyder.
p. cm.
ISBN 0-7643-1151-4 (hardcover)
1. Hull Pottery Company--Catalogs. 2. Pottery--20th century--Collectors and collecting--Ohio--Crooksville--Catalogs. I. title.
NK4210.H84 A4 2001
738.3'09771'59--dc21   00-009075

Designed by "Sue"
Type set in Zapf Chancery Bd BT/Korinna BT

ISBN: 0-7643-1151-4
Printed in China
1 2 3 4

Published by Schiffer Publishing Ltd.
4880 Lower Valley Road
Atglen, PA 19310
Phone: (610) 593-1777; Fax: (610) 593-2002
E-mail: Schifferbk@aol.com
Please visit our web site catalog at
www.schifferbooks.com
We are always looking for people to write books on new and related subjects. If you have an idea for a book please contact us at the above address.

This book may be purchased from the publisher.
Include $3.95 for shipping.
Please try your bookstore first.
You may write for a free catalog.

In Europe, Schiffer books are distributed by
Bushwood Books
6 Marksbury Ave.
Kew Gardens
Surrey TW9 4JF England
Phone: 44 (0)208 392-8585
Fax: 44 (0)208 392-9876
E-mail: Bushwd@aol.com
Free postage in the UK. Europe: air mail at cost

Acknowledgments

I would like to thank everyone who contributed to this book; all of the dealers and collectors who generously opened their homes and shops to me. They provided me with collections, invaluable insights and information that only comes from many years of diligent searching and passionate involvement with Hull ceramics and its history. My thanks go out to Lyle Applegate, Thomas F. and Heather A. Evans, Michael and Sharon Reinheimer, and Betty and Joe Yonis. Your cooperation and hospitality made the job worthwhile.

I would also like to thank those people who kindly offered to open their collections to me but who I was unable to visit as time ran out. Your offers were truly appreciated!

Every collector needs a friendly group of like-minded people to turn to for advice, information, and camaraderie. The members of the Hull Pottery Association are just such a group. To learn more about the Association, or to join, call Betty and Joe Yonis in Ohio at 740-982-6763.

Finally, I thank the readers. Without you, this book would not be possible.

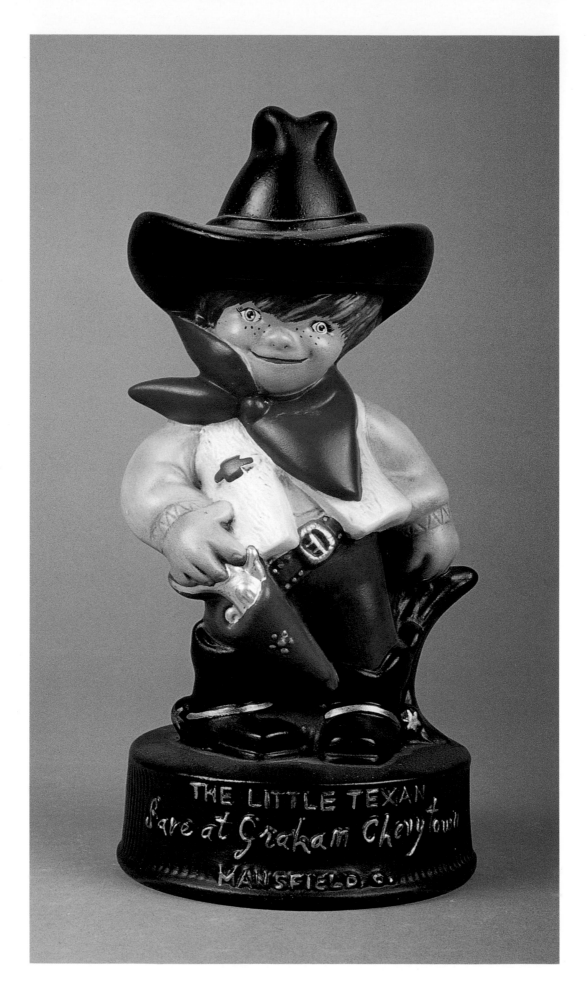

Contents

Introduction

Early Hull mug, bearing the company's circle H mark and the number 499, 5" high. *Courtesy of the Collection of Betty and Joe Yonis.* $55-60

Hull pottery could be found in daily use in American homes throughout much of the twentieth century. The A. E. Hull Pottery Company, formed in July 1905 in Crooksville, Ohio, and later renamed the Hull Pottery Company, produced a wide variety of wares to fill an equally wide variety of purposes. Collectors today are discovering what twentieth-century consumers learned the first time around: whatever pottery was needed or desired, there was likely to be ware from Hull to fill that need.

Collectors today are discovering what twentieth-century consumers learned the first time around: whatever pottery was needed or desired, there was likely to be ware from Hull to fill that need. Early stoneware salt box excavated from beneath the Hull factory. 6" diameter x 4" high. *Courtesy of the Collection of Betty and Joe Yonis.* $250-275

Opposite page:
An imaginative novelty piece made by Hull Pottery by combining a novelty donkey planter and an altered "Swing Band" drummer novelty figure. This donkey rider and his mount, produced originally for President Franklin D. Roosevelt, measure 7.5" high x 7" long. *Courtesy of the Collection of Betty and Joe Yonis.* $2200-2420

Right:
Artware pitcher decorated in the Tulip (Sueno) motif, 109-33, 13" high. *Courtesy of Michael and Sharon Reinheimer* $385-425

Miniature vases decorated in a variety of artware motifs. These small vases range in height from 4" to 5" high. *Courtesy of the Collection of Betty and Joe Yonis.* Diminutive vases range in value from $75-150.

Corky Pig piggy banks with colorful glazes. Corky Pigs were first produced by Hull in 1957 and would continue to be produced throughout the active life of the firm. 8" & 7" sizes. *Courtesy of Michael and Sharon Reinheimer.* Left to right: $175-190; $150-165; $125-135

These swans were part of the Imperial line, "Designed Especially for Florists." "Florist wares" under the Imperial name were first offered in 1955. Swan planters/centerpieces, F812, 8" high x 9" long. For the Imperial line, Hull conveniently added an "F" to the item numbers. As seen here, throughout this book when the item number for a particular piece is known, it will be included immediately after the description of the piece and before any measurements. *Courtesy of Michael and Sharon Reinheimer.* Left to right, swans in glazes: Tangerine, $50-55; Agate, $40-45; White, $25-30; Brown, $100-110; Butterscotch, $50-55

The House 'n Garden Rainbow Servingware line was introduced in 1961. The four Rainbow glaze colors are shown. The Mirror Brown glaze color shown on the left hand plate, cup and saucer, were first offered (with the introduction of the House 'n Garden line) in 1960. *Courtesy of the Collection of Betty and Joe Yonis.* $100-110 per set.

Many American pottery firms in the nineteenth and early twentieth centuries first entered the ceramics market by offering eminently practical stonewares designed for daily use. Hull was no exception. Among the company's earliest offering (from 1905 on into the 1930s) were sturdy stonewares in many forms, both plain and decorative. Hull stonewares, ranging from utilitarian and kitchenwares to toilet sets and jardinieres, are as attractive as they are durable. They are often decorated with a variety of molded patterns and covered in striking, yet simple glazes. Stonewares today remain among pottery's hidden treasures. They are often overlooked in favor of more delicate and intricate earthenwares and porcelains. Still, they have a simple and enduring charm that is soon to be discovered.

Stoneware.
Early Hull flower pot. 7.5" diameter x 6" high. Marked with H in circle. *Courtesy of the Collection of Betty and Joe Yonis.* $275-300

Around 1907, Hull began to diversify, providing domestic, hotel, and restaurant wares—ranging from kitchenwares to sanitary wares—in a strong white earthenware known as semi-porcelain. In the early 1930s, consumers were first introduced to the convenience of "ovenproof" kitchenwares, items both sturdy and attractive enough that they could be taken from the oven directly to the table without embarrassing the host or hostess. Such wares proved to be very popular with American consumers. By the mid-to-late 1930s, Hull began adding their contributions to these ovenproof kitchenwares with a wide range of innovative serving pieces. Accompanying these were attractive canister sets, cookie jars, bowls and shakers.

One of Hull's contributions to ovenproof kitchenware: Cinderella Blossom, 1948-1949. Shakers and creamer. *Courtesy of Michael and Sharon Reinheimer.* Shakers: $25-30 pair; creamer: $15-16

Imperial Florist Wares.
Mirror Brown planters. Left to right: experimental piece, 7.75" high; footed planter, B31, 5.25" high; pedestal vase with lion handles, F64, 6.75" high; planter, F55, 4" high x 5.75" wide. *Courtesy of Michael and Sharon Reinheimer.* Experimental, $125-135; B31, $45-50; F64, $75-85; F55, $40-45

Imperial Florist Wares.
Bird planters: chickadee (tail down), F474; chickadee (tail up), F473; penguin, F472. *Courtesy of Michael and Sharon Reinheimer.* F474, $20-25; F473, $20-25; F472, $40-45

Over the decades, Hull would add a wide range of artwares, "florist wares" (ranging from flower pots to planters and jardinieres), and cheery novelty items to their product lines. The artwares reflect the varying stylistic trends of the passing decades. The floral and novelty items come in a wide variety of forms, some very imaginative and playful. As demand for artware declined in the marketplace, Hull turned to the production of florist wares with enthusiasm. Many of these wares are part of the company's Imperial line.

Novlety.
Two cat novelty planters, 11" high. *Courtesy of the Collection of Betty and Joe Yonis.* $125-135 each

In 1960, Hull Pottery introduced the House 'n Garden "Serving-ware" line, featuring tablewares of all sorts. The House 'n Garden line featured heavy forms with simple lines. These practical services were perfectly suited for use day in and day out, both inside or outside, in causal settings from family dinners in front of the television to a barbecue with friends. Over one hundred different pieces were produced during House 'n Garden's twenty-five year production run. Various Serving-wares would continue to be produced until, faced with severe overseas competition and internal disputes, the Hull Pottery Company was forced to close in 1986.

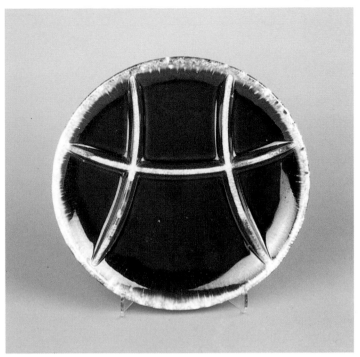

House 'n Garden Ovenproof Serving-ware.
Rare Hull Mirror Brown divided grill plate, with the letter H dividing the plate, 9.5" diameter *Courtesy of Michael and Sharon Reinheimer.* $150-165

Left:
House 'n Garden Ovenproof Serving-ware.
Chip and dip set glazed in Mirror Brown, trimmed with an Ivory foam edge, and finished with a metal handle. *Courtesy of Lyle Applegate.* $75-85

Packaging and shipping Hull Ovenproof Serving-ware could be a simple and direct process. *Courtesy of Michael and Sharon Reinheimer.* NP (**N**o **P**rice)

What follows is a survey of the varied wares produced by the prolific Hull Pottery Company throughout much of the twentieth century.

Rarities

Rare Hull Pottery pieces, sample and experimental items, and wares used to produce and decorate Hull pottery are joys to discover. When found, *unique* items—produced and/or decorated by employees for themselves, their loved ones, or their friends— give a collector unlimited bragging rights. Here are a few of the items encountered on the road.

A rare George and Martha Washington figure set designed by Warren Garrett. 5" high x 5" long each. *Courtesy of the Collection of Betty and Joe Yonis.* $600-660

Left and below:
Rare unmarked "bird taking wing" flower frog sold with this leaf dish. Bird flower frog, 10.5" high. Leaf dish, 85, 13" long. *Courtesy of the Collection of Betty and Joe Yonis.* Flower frog, $100-110; dish, $60-70

Sample vase in the Starfire pattern (never produced) and a sample candleholder. 8" & 4" high respectively. *Courtesy of the Collection of Betty and Joe Yonis.* Starfire, $1600-1760; candleholder, $300-330

Experimental white rabbit candy box. 7.5" long x 7" high at ear tips. This piece was never released into mass-production. *Courtesy of the Collection of Betty and Joe Yonis.* $500-550. In brown: $750-825.

Above and right:
Two experimental pieces —the company was testing various glaze colors— that never made it into production. Left: a soup and sandwich set (tray and soup mug) with unusual glazing; right: a Crestone pitcher in Mirror Brown glazing. *Courtesy of Michael and Sharon Reinheimer.* Left: $25-30; right: $50-55

Glaze paint cups used within the plant, 3.5" high x 3" diameter. The gray cup is marked with an incised number code: 2-11-175V-20-. *Courtesy of Michael and Sharon Reinheimer.* $15-20 each

Two experimental pieces: the cookie jar measures 9.75" high. *Courtesy of Michael and Sharon Reinheimer.* Cookie jar, $175-190; casserole, $75-85

Right and below:
Fat Thorne made this unique bear at Hull in 1931. *Courtesy of the Collection of Betty and Joe Yonis.* $500-550

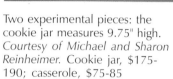

Above and right:
Lion by Fat Thorne,
produced in an
earthenware body.
5.25" long. *Courtesy of
the Collection of Betty
and Joe Yonis.* $200-
220

Left and above:
Miniature spittoon, dated 1945,
employee made sample. Date
and employee's initials incised.
*Courtesy of the Collection of
Betty and Joe Yonis.* $250-275

A typical open front vase shape (made by Vesta Watts) used in the Continental artware line (1959-1960), the Imperial florist ware line, and others, specially decorated by Gladys Showers. Mrs. Showers was a Hull Pottery Company nurse who specialized in porcelain decoration. She also made a doll that is very well known in the doll collecting community. Vase: 10.25" high. *Courtesy of the Collection of Betty and Joe Yonis.* $250-275

Below:
Three pieces decorated at the Ohio Ceramic Center after the Hull Pottery Company had shut down. Unfinished blanks were decorated by Nancy Dennis. She also decorated some quite elaborate scenes and floral sprays on some of the blanks. *Courtesy of Michael and Sharon Reinheimer.* $50-55 each

Ware Types and Decorations

Before becoming immersed in this survey of the history of the firm and the many different Hull wares, it is useful to take a few minutes and define some terms. Generally speaking, Hull produced pottery with three different body types. The company's earliest wares were "stonewares," which are hard, high-fired wares that are opaque and non-porous (stonewares do not require a glaze coating to be waterproof). The stoneware body (below the glaze) is usually gray, buff or brown in color. During the earlier years of production, Hull also produced "yellow ware." Yellow ware has a yellow-gold or buff-yellow body color. Yellow wares tend to be kitchenwares and chamber pots and, in many cases, are given a clear glaze coating that allows the yellow color of the body to show through. Much of the ware produced by Hull, however, is "semi-porcelain," a hard, white-bodied ware type used for everything from kitchen and Serving-wares to artwares and florist lines.

Hull pottery was decorated in many ways. The wares were cast in molds and many items feature molded decorations. These molded decorations are part of the mold itself. As the mold shapes the vessel, it shapes the molded decorations into the clay as well. Additionally, Hull pottery was generally decorated with a wide variety of colored glazes. Glaze is made up of minute particles of colored or clear glass suspended in a liquid carrying agent and is applied by dipping, brushing, or airbrushing. Glazes are fired after they are applied, creating a glass-like protective and decorative coating over the clay body. This glaze coating also renders porous earthenware clay bodies waterproof. Glaze can have either a gloss or matte finish.

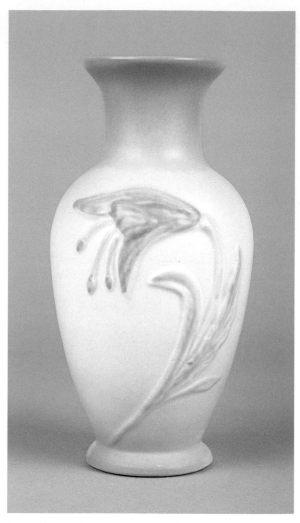

Matte glaze colors were employed to decorate this Classic vase, dating from 1942-1945. 6.75" high. *Courtesy of the Collection of Betty and Joe Yonis.* $250-275

Hull pottery wares were cast in molds and many featured molded decorations, including these Gingerbread Man cookie jars. These cookie jars are also glazed in three different glossy glaze colors. 11.25" high. *Courtesy of Michael and Sharon Reinheimer.* Left to right: $500-550; $200-220; $450-495

Hand painted decorations could have been applied to Hull pottery either under the glaze, over the glaze, or both. Underglaze hand painted decorations were applied prior to the glazing and firing of the bisque (bisque is a fired clay body, hardened but as yet unglazed). The colors used in underglaze decoration must be able to withstand the high temperatures required for glaze firing. When vessels are decorated with underglaze painting, the surface reflects light evenly.

Overglaze hand painting, on the other hand, involved colors applied after the glazing and firing was done, as these colors would not survive the high temperatures involved in glazing. Colors applied over the glaze were generally set in place in a low-fired glost oven. Items decorated with overglaze paints will not reflect light evenly in the painted areas. Overglaze enamels may wear away with time and use. It is possible to detect where overglaze colors have worn away, as the glaze is left with a matte surface in the formerly decorated areas.

A fine example of underglaze hand painted floral decoration is shown on the side of this Jumbo Corky Pig. This piggy bank, 197, measures 8" high. *Courtesy of the Collection of Betty and Joe Yonis.* $500-550

Two piggy banks with different overglaze "cold paint" floral motifs, produced in the 1940s. 14" long. *Courtesy of the Collection of Betty and Joe Yonis.* $150-165 each

Some objects may also feature a combination of both hand painted overglaze and underglaze decorations. Each decorative technique would receive a separate firing as demanded by the paint.

Another decorative technique employed by Hull in the company's early years was decalcomania. Decalcomania is a printed decoration. The print is transferred from a colorful decal to the surface of the ceramic with the use of specially prepared transfer paper. Decalcomania patterns tend to be floral motifs used as either a central pattern or as a border.

Gilt was also used by Hull to add a finishing touch at times. There are various gilt mixtures, containing gold, that could be painted onto selected portions of an object. Once applied, the gilt was then fired and burnished to create a shiny gold decoration. When gilt is worn away, as happens through frequent use and repeated washing, it leaves behind dull spots in the glaze. Gilt was often employed in combination with either hand painted or decalcomania designs.

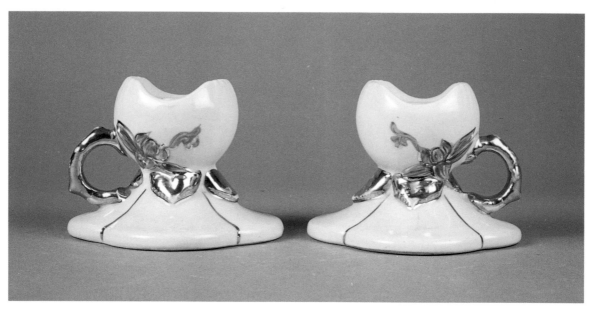

Woodland, New Gloss, 1949-1950, candleholders embellished with gold gilt decoration. W30, 3.5" high. *Courtesy of the Collection of Betty and Joe Yonis.* $60-70 pair.

Methods of Production

Hull pottery was mass-produced, using a variety of sectional plaster cast molds to shape the pottery. Mass-produced pottery was usually formed in one of three ways: by *jiggering*, *hand casting*, or *ram pressing*. *Jiggering* could either be done by hand or automatically. Jiggering uses a machine with a revolving mold to produce flatwares such as plates. The mold formed the inside of the plate while the "shoe" formed the outside and foot ring. The shoe itself is manufactured in the shape desired for the outside or underside of the pottery piece. The "jiggerman" threw the clay "bat" and worked it up in the mold by hand and then pressed the shoe (also called the "profile") down onto the clay to form the piece. Excess clay was cut away. At this point the mold was removed from the jigger wheel to dry overnight. Once the clay was dry, the piece was removed from the mold and the

mold was reused. This process has been automated for the creation of smaller ceramic forms. All of the steps are accomplished by machine in automatic jiggering. (Cushion 1974, 163; Snyder 1999a, 17-18)

Hollow form pottery items, such as cookie jars, may be produced by *hand casting*. In this process, a mold is filled with clay slip. After around twenty minutes, the mold is drained, preventing the creation of a solid cookie jar. What remains within the mold after draining is the clay that set up along the wall of the mold during those first twenty minutes. This clay measures roughly 3/16" in thickness. If the clay slip was allowed to remain in the mold longer, more of the slip would set up and the walls of the hollow form vessel would be thicker. Ceramic pieces of any shape or size could be cast using this method, although the process was usually limited to two to three part molds.

Unlike hand casting, clay used in *ram pressing* was very stiff. A hydraulic ram press was used to mechanically close and open simple two piece molds around the clay. When the press opened, the formed clay piece was removed. Once Hull pottery was removed from the sectional molds, whether ram pressed or hand cast, and before it was fired, mold seam lines left behind on the ware were trimmed away. Some of the more complex artware forms required extra skill and care in trimming.(Snyder 1999a, 17-18; Roberts 1980, 12)

Two methods standard in the potting industry were employed by Hull to keep the glazes from sticking to the sagger (a protective pottery shell surrounding ceramics in the kiln) as they hardened during firing. In cases where glaze covers the base of the ware, Hull pottery was raised off the sagger using small, three pronged stilts. A stilt is a small, Y shaped bisque support, a type of "kiln furniture," with projections reaching up above and down below the Y. As the glaze hardened during firing, it would adhere to the three slender ends of the stilt prongs in contact with the glazed surface. Once the firing was complete, and the kiln cooled, it was a simple matter, however, to snap the thin stilt prongs loose and then grind down the remaining prong fragments. Once ground down, three small unglazed dots were all that was left behind to indicate where the stilt prongs had supported the piece. These tiny unglazed areas should not be mistaken for damage to the pottery. They are artifacts of the production method and do not decrease the value of the ceramics.

Alternatively, much Hull pottery was produced with a "dry foot," a raised area of the base that was carefully left unglazed and supported the ceramic in the sagger during firing. Like the stilt, the dry foot kept the glaze from coming into contact with the surrounding sagger, making sure the glaze stuck only to the pot and not to the surrounding kiln furniture. (Snyder 1999a, 17-18)

A good example of a dry foot. *Courtesy of the Collection of Betty and Joe Yonis; courtesy of Thomas F. and Heather A. Evans.*

Note the three stilt marks around the inner edge of the foot ring. *Courtesy of the Collection of Betty and Joe Yonis.*

Factory Flaws

It is also worthwhile to take a moment to become familiar with the most common types of factory flaws and to be able to quickly distinguish these from evidence of damage inflicted upon a piece after it has left the factory. While these factory flaws will lower the value of the wares they occur on, they do not reduce value nearly as much as damage incurred later on. Pieces with manufacturing flaws should not be considered damaged goods.

Pottery production, like life itself, does not always go smoothly. Mistakes are made and some pottery is produced with small irregularities. Depending on the standards of the potting firm involved, wares featuring small irregularities may have been overlooked entirely or they may have been sold as factory seconds.

Common factory flaws include unusual glaze color variations, thin spots in the glaze, visible mold seam lines, uneven bases, ill-fitting lids, and handles that do not match in proportion or placement. At times, pottery chipped in the bisque stage was glazed and fired anyway. On close inspection you will note in this case that the glaze completely covers the break. Along this line, pots have at times been glazed and fired with small bits of clay adhering to an otherwise smooth surface. These clay bits should have been removed prior to glazing and firing, but were missed by the potter. Finally, "kiln kisses" occur when a pot touches either the sagger wall or another pot as it is being loaded into the sagger for firing, leaving dents or unglazed areas on the pot. (Bassett 1999, 18)

Orchid, 1939-1941. Basket, 305. The handle broke off during production in the factory and workers smoothed down the breaks and glazed them over to make this unique piece. Shown with the complete vase. 4.75" high without handle. 7" high with handle. *Courtesy of the Collection of Betty and Joe Yonis.* Handleless, $400-440; with handle, $550-600

Factoring in variances in materials and production methods, Hull pottery—though mass-produced—was not entirely precise. Sizes and capacities are not always exact. Small variations are common. All pottery from every firm would feature such variations, to greater or lesser degrees depending on each firm's quality control measures.

Crazing — A Separate Issue

Glaze crazing is another common flaw. However crazing will occur both in the factory and over time. In the factory, crazing takes place when the clay body and glaze cool at different rates, creating thin cracks in the glaze. Crazing also occurs when the body of the ceramic ware shrinks over time. The stiff, glass-like glaze cannot follow this reduction in body size and glaze cracks appear. While not damaging to the structure of the pot, crazing will increase with age. Crazing often develops on tableware after repeated reheating in the oven. (Schneider 1991, 14-15)

The A.E. Hull Pottery Company addressed the issue of crazing in wares after they had left the factory. The firm's management stated that it was beyond their abilities to create earthenware that would not eventually craze. They reserved the right to refuse to compensate merchants for crazed items the company deemed to have remained in stock too long. (Roberts 1980, 9)

If you are seeking out the more common Hull wares, you can afford to pass over heavily crazed pieces and wait for something better. Use your best judgment when it comes to less common or rare items.

Manufacturer's Marks

Manufacturer's marks are quite useful in the immediate identification and dating of the wares from a particular pottery firm. As years go by, a pottery company is quite likely to change the style of the marks employed. When the dates of these changes are well known, it is possible to identify the period in which a pot bearing a particular mark was made.

In many cases, further identification is possible with Hull. In the mid-1930s, the company provided specific designation numbers to a number of their wares. Two digit item prefix numbers were used to identify Hull pottery made in a stoneware body. Three digit item prefix numbers were used for semi-porcelain earthenware bodies. Artwares often included these designations, along with convenient enumeration of the size of each form.

What follows is a sampling of the various Hull marks to be found on the company's wares. For a more detailed review of Hull's marks, see Brenda Roberts *Roberts' Ultimate Encyclopedia of Hull Pottery.*

Molded Hull U.S.A. mark, introduced c. 1938 and used frequently on Hull artwares. This example includes the item number and size. Sizes, diameter s, or heights (as appropriate) frequently accompany this mark and others. *Courtesy of the Collection of Betty and Joe Yonis.*

Foil Hull Pottery label featuring a potter-at-wheel logo. This label appeared on many of Hull's artwares of the 1940s. The lettering may be found in gold, silver, or gray. This mark would go on to be used on company advertising and letterhead after 1950. *Courtesy of Michael and Sharon Reinheimer.*

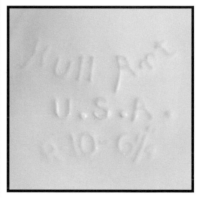

Molded and incised Hull Art U.S.A. marks in use in the 1940s. Once again, these examples also feature the item numbers and sizes. *Courtesy of the Collection of Betty and Joe Yonis; courtesy of Michael and Sharon Reinheimer.*

The incised H in a circle mark was in use in the 1920s and continued on into the 1930s. Early examples have a far bolder H than those shown here. Mold and size numbers frequently accompany this mark. *Courtesy of the Collection of Betty and Joe Yonis.*

Incised Hull Ovenserve U.S.A. mark appearing on the Cinderella line. This mark was used for both the Cinderella Blossom and Bouquet motifs. The Cinderella line was in use during 1948-1949. *Courtesy of Michael and Sharon Reinheimer.*

Incised H P CO U.S.A. mark with Corky Pig trademark, Pat Pend, and 1957 date. Corky Pigs would continued in use through the 1980s. *Courtesy of Lyle Applegate.*

Regal mark. The Regal line was offered to chain stores by Hull Pottery from 1952 to 1960. *Courtesy of Michael and Sharon Reinheimer.*

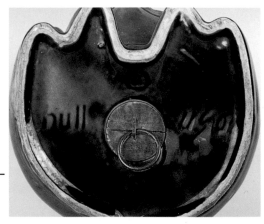

Incised lower case hull and italicised USA mark in use on both House 'n Garden and Imperial lines of the 1960s (Imperial precedes House 'n Garden, first offered in 1955). This mark also appears on this novelty piggy bank.

Inscribed script Hull USA marks used for both artware and kitchenware lines during the 1950s. Such marks were also molded. The first example, with incised blue lines and the T2 item number, was used on the Blossom Flite artware line produced from 1955-1956. The other three examples appeared on the 1957-1958 Fiesta and Heritageware lines. *Courtesy of the Collection of Betty and Joe Yonis.*

Hull's Coronet mark. The Coronet line was sold to chain stores in 1959. *Courtesy of Thomas F. and Heather A. Evans.*

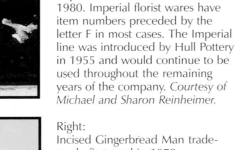

Imperial mark in use from 1960 to 1980. Imperial florist wares have item numbers preceded by the letter F in most cases. The Imperial line was introduced by Hull Pottery in 1955 and would continue to be used throughout the remaining years of the company. *Courtesy of Michael and Sharon Reinheimer.*

Right:
Incised Gingerbread Man trademark, first used in 1978.

Circular, incised Crestone mark in use from 1965 to 1967.

Left and below:
These marks, including the Crooksville, Ohio, location, was in use on Hull dinnerware lines from 1982-1985. Note the change from Oven Proof to Oven & Microwave between these two marks. *Courtesy of the Collection of Betty and Joe Yonis; courtesy of Thomas F. and Heather A. Evans.*

Left:
This incised hull Ovenproof USA mark was in use from 1960 through 1986 when the plant closed. The black rectangular foil label precedes this mark, introduced in 1958, first used on novelty and florist ware lines.

This incised script Serving Tray OvenProof hull U.S.A. mark was first used in c. 1978, although the earliest serving trays were unmarked. Note the small piece of extra clay that was not removed from the lower left inside edge of the tray's foot rim prior to the glaze firing. This is a wonderful illustration of a factory flaw.

History of the Company and its Wares

A look back at the old A.E. Hull Pottery Company facility. A modern stoneware plate commemorating the A.E. Hull Pottery Company produced by Robinson Ransbottom—a pottery works still producing stoneware in Roseville, Ohio, at the time this book was first written. The mark reads "Robinson Ransbottom Pottery / Roseville, Ohio U.S.A." *Courtesy of the Collection of Betty and Joe Yonis.* $150-200

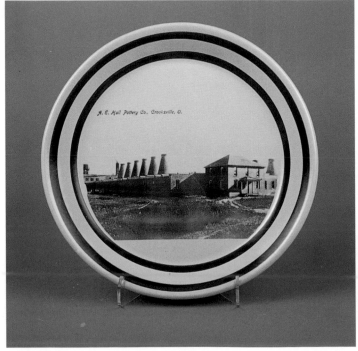

The history of the firm and its many wares have been divided into three general periods of production. These periods are based loosely upon the changing character of the wares produced by Hull during these three periods and will be discussed in detail below. The company's earliest years (1905-1930) deal largely with the firm's production of utilitarian stonewares and their early production of semi-porcelains. Both stonewares and semi-porcelains were offered for the home, and for the restaurant and hotel trades. This is the period in which the company also introduced artwares into their product lines. The middle years (1930-1960) begin with the passing of the company from Addis Hull to his son. This period includes the vast majority of the artwares and novelty pieces collectors are familiar with: the imaginatively molded and beautifully glazed decorative wares so popular throughout this era. The later years (1960-1986) begin with the introduction of both the House 'n Garden casual serving/dinnerware lines and the flourishing of the Imperial florist wares (flower pots, planters, and other items suited for the florist trade first introduced to the public in 1955). This last period ends with the company's closure.

While these three periods help to organize the vast quantities of wares produced by Hull, they are simply guidelines. Products introduced during either the early or middle periods may extend well beyond the end of that period. Some items remained popular for many years to come. However, using the years of introduction as our guide, it is easier to chart the company's changes in style and emphasis over the many decades of production.

Early Company History and Wares, 1905-1930

Addis Emmet Hull was no newcomer to the pottery game when he established the pottery company that bore his name. He came from a potting family; his brother, J.J. Hull, had owned and operated the Star Stonery Company, providing stonewares from the Mississippi to the East Coast, since 1892. After peddling his brother's stonewares for a time, Addis E. Hull first tried his hand at producing these durable and popular wares in 1901, establishing and operating the Globe Stoneware Company. Selling his interest in the Globe in 1904, Addis Hull founded his A.E. Hull Pottery Company in Crooksville, Ohio, in July of 1905.

The location was right. Crooksville is located in eastern Ohio, an area rich with the natural resources necessary to the production of pottery (i.e. clay and fossil fuels) — and hence, rich with pottery firms. The towns of Crooksville, Roseville, Zanesville, and — further to the north and east — East Liverpool all had their share of thriving pottery establishments. Experienced potting talent was available in abundance. Addis Hull quickly drew personnel from both the Star and Globe potteries to help staff his new venture, a four kiln single plant operation located on China Street. Under these conditions, it was not long before the A.E. Hull Pottery Company was well known for the production of quality stonewares and stoneware specialties.

J.J. Hull was no slouch either. While Addis was developing his stoneware potteries, J.J. had turned to the manufacture of semi-porcelains. His Star Stonery Company's stonewares had been useful in many largely utilitarian ways; however, semi-porcelains lent themselves to a much wider range of uses ... and a much broader consumer market. Along with several business partners, J.J. Hull established the Acme Pottery Company in 1903, producing semi-porcelain dinnerwares, both decorated and plain.

In 1907, the A.E. Hull Pottery Company purchased the Acme Pottery, adding both a second plant to their operation and the diversity semi-porcelains could provide to their product lines. This move obviously strengthened the firm. By the early 1920s, the company would have branch offices in New York, Chicago and Detroit along with a warehouse facility in Jersey City, New Jersey and would be producing a full range of utilitarian and kitchenwares, accompanied by florist and garden pots/jardinieres. (Konyah 1999, 123; Roberts 1980, 6-10)

For the Kitchen, Home, Restaurant and Hotel: Hull's Early Production

From its inception, the A. E. Hull Pottery Company produced a wide range of stoneware forms in great numbers. Early utilitarian stonewares included a vast array of butter jars, dairy jugs, milk pans, meat tubs, preserve jars, water jugs and kegs, to name a few. For use in the kitchen, Hull stonewares included nested bowls, nappy sets (sauce dishes generally used to serve stewed fruit, applesauce, and similar foods), and salt boxes. Cuspidors and basins and ewers were produced for use elsewhere around the house. Early artwares and jardinieres were also available. (Snyder 1995)

These early stonewares were produced plain or with molded (embossed) decorations. Among the many embossed patterns to be found on early Hull stonewares are fruit, flowers, fowl, animals ranging from cattle to stags, children, castles, fishscale and fleur-de-lis patterns, harps, and hearts and arrows. A variety of glaze colors were used on Hull's early stonewares, including solid blues, black and white, browns, greens, and grays. Blended and mottled glazes were also employed to good effect in both high gloss and matte finishes. Overglaze banding, decals, and stamped decorations also added to the variety of appearances available in early stonewares. Some of these would persist well on into the 1930s.

Stoneware.
Pretzel jar with circle H mark, lid missing, 7.5" high base.
Courtesy of Michael and Sharon Reinheimer. $250-275

Early Hull blue banded pitcher marked with the H in circle, 4.75"
high. *Courtesy of Michael and Sharon Reinheimer.* $50-55

Stoneware.
Pitcher, stein and mug with circle H mark: the pitcher measures 9.5"
high. *Courtesy of Michael and Sharon Reinheimer.* Pitcher, $150-
165; stein, $35-40; mug, $35-40

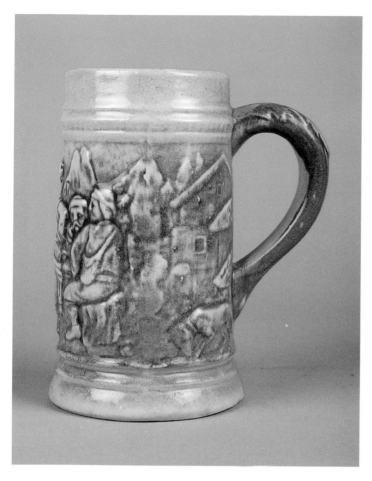

Stoneware.
Stein, 6.25" high. *Courtesy of the Collection of Betty and Joe Yonis.*
$55-60

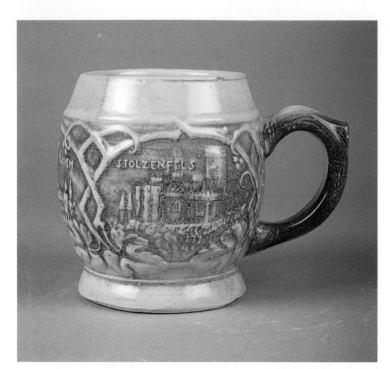

Stoneware.
Early mug, 497, with H in circle mark. Along with the Germanic scenes are the names/words: "Rhein Stein, Burg, Cochem, Stolzenfels." 4.5" high.
Courtesy of the Collection of Betty and Joe Yonis.
$45-50

Early Hull pitcher and mugs with the H in circle mark. Decorated on one side only. Pitcher, 6.5" high; mugs, 4.5" high. *Courtesy of the Collection of Betty and Joe Yonis.* $150-165 set; mugs, $40-45 each

The baby's needs were not forgotten. Early nursery wares were offered from 1920 to 1932. Included among these predominantly semi-porcelain forms were bread and milk sets, deep baby plates, cups and saucers, and mugs.

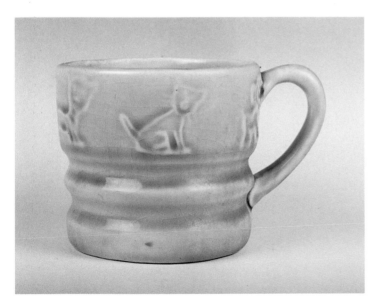

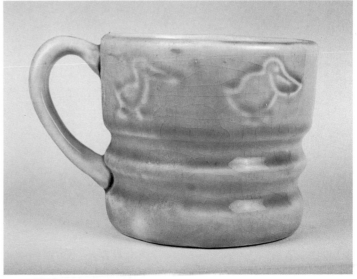

Nursery Wares.
Child's mug with animals all around. 3" high. *Courtesy of the Collection of Betty and Joe Yonis.* $125-135

By 1920, stoneware pedestaled jardinieres were introduced into the Hull lines and would remain in production for more than a decade. The jardinieres themselves ranged in size from 5" to 10" in diameter and the pedestals that supported them were 16" to 18" high. These were offered in a variety of glaze colors and made impressive displays for potted plants.

In 1920, Addis Hull also oversaw his company's importation of inexpensive European pottery into the country through his Jersey City warehouse. The wares were not marked as being Hull products and this venture ceased in 1929 with the onset of America's Depression years. (Roberts 1980, pp. 19-23; Roberts 1992, pp. 68-78)

Early Artwares

In the 1920s, Hull began producing artwares and dabbled with tiles. For over a decade beginning in 1925, the firm produced artwares in both semi-porcelains and stonewares. Among these decorative, yet useful items suitable for the home and garden were hanging baskets, bulb bowls, flower pots and saucers, jardinieres and vases. The company's early artwares were glazed in solid colors including the matte colors Lotus Blue, Autumn Brown, Bermuda Green, Egyptian Green, Eggshell White, Oyster White, and Maize Yellow (among other fanciful glaze names). Striking matte and high gloss blended glaze combinations were employed to create a different effect.

Examples of Hull's early artwares included a line of Lusterware and a stoneware Tulip line. The lusterwares were glazed in a number of bright, iridescent colors. Over thirty-five items were offered in these lustrous glazes. The Tulip line featured a floral motif self-evident in the name embossed on stoneware jardinieres, the pedestals that supported them, and on vases. Behind the tulips, the background glaze was a deep brown. At times the interiors of these vessels were glazed in white. The flowers themselves were at times decorated with overglaze cold paint colors.

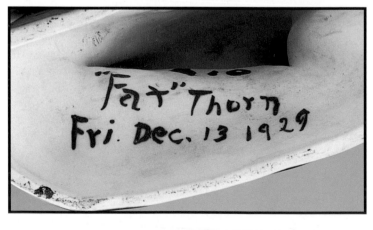

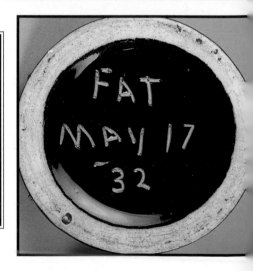

Right: Fat Thorne Lusterware-style candleholders with hand painted decoration, dated May 17, 1932. 3" high. *Courtesy of the Collection of Betty and Joe Yonis.* $200-220

Fat Thorne doorstop horse, made in 1929. *Courtesy of the Collection of Betty and Joe Yonis.* $750-825

Old Spice.
After shave & talcum powder bottles and shaving mug. The bottles are marked in the banner Ship Grand Turk; the mug is marked in the banner Ship Friendship. 5.5" bottle (with stopper), 5.25" bottle (without stopper), 3" high mug. Note the Shulton paper label on the bottom of the stoppered after shave bottle. *Courtesy of Michael and Sharon Reinheimer.* $20-35 each

From c. 1926 to the early 1930s, Hull produced tiles, either plain or faience. Most of the company's tile business was on a special order basis, with many orders being placed from Chicago, Detroit, and New York. Decorative Hull tiles graced the fireplace mantles, floors, and walls of many homes during this period. High gloss and matte finishes were applied to these tiles in either solid or stippled treatments. Hull also offered accessory pieces, soap dishes and towel racks, in complementary glaze colors. (Roberts 1980, 9)

Middle Years and Wares, 1930-1950s

With Addis Hull's death in 1930, his son, Addis E. Hull, Jr., took over the company reins and brought the firm through the difficult Depression years. The company continued to produced its utilitarian forms and kitchenwares, along with the florist and garden pots/jar-

dinieres, in the late 1930s. However, the firm also turned to the production of much greater quantities of artwares (designed by an accomplished artisan with glazes formulated by experts, then mass-produced and glazed by accomplished laborers) in motifs most familiar to (and sought by) seasoned collectors.

Two notable events occurred in the A.E. Hull Pottery Company's history in 1937. In production, the firm began, under contract, to manufacture ceramic cosmetic containers for men with the Shulton company of New York. Better known among these wares were the Old Spice shaving mugs and Old Spice bottles for men's cologne, after shave lotion, and after shave talc. Shulton introduced their Old Spice line in Hull containers the following year. Initial manly amusement in the industry over the introduction of notions and lotions for men was quickly dispelled as Shulton's sales of Old Spice men's products quickly outsold their women's lines. Hull Pottery would supply Shulton with containers until 1944.

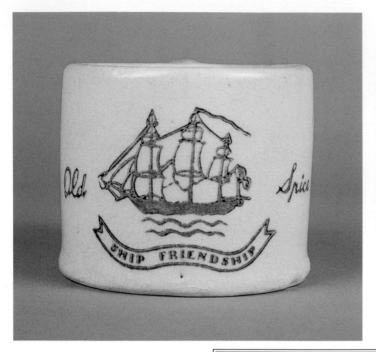 

Old Spice shaving mug, 3" high. *Courtesy of the Collection of Betty and Joe Yonis.* $30-35

The second notable event occurred in management with the resignation of Addis E. Hull, Jr. in 1937. He left the company his father had founded to take charge of the nearby Shawnee Pottery Company of Zanesville, Ohio. With his departure, Gerald F. Watts took control at Hull. The transition was apparently a smooth one and production of the company's most popular artware lines began in earnest in the following year.

Artwares

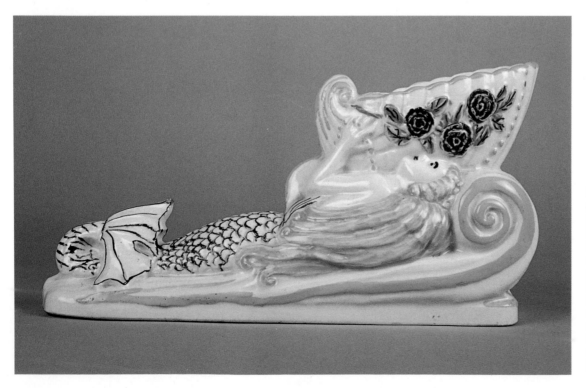

Mermaid/Shell planter decorated in the Open Rose motif, hand painted by Hull employee Jean Heskett. This Open Rose artware item, with this particular hand painted decoration, is unique. Mass-produced examples of this mermaid, with more ordinary decoration, are found. *Courtesy of the Collection of Betty and Joe Yonis.* $3000-3300

The company's artware lines included vases, baskets, bowls, ewers, candleholders, rose bowls and wall pockets. Tea sets were many times produced in the same decorative motifs as the artware lines, with complimentary forms. Often the hollow wares (baskets, bowls, ewers, and vases) were made in graduated sizes. While the decorative motifs were distinctive for each artware line, lines often shared the same body shapes between them.

Hull's Artware: A Sampler

The dates provided here should not be considered to be absolute. There is always the possibility that new research will alter dating. Such is the nature of humanity's pursuit of the past. Historians and researchers of all stripes have found "the past" to be an astoundingly agile and elusive opponent! For further information concerning Hull's artwares, see Brenda Roberts, *Roberts' Ultimate Encyclopedia of Hull Pottery.*

Crab Apple	1934-1935
Calla Lily	1938-1940
Thistle	1938-1941
Tulip	1938-1941
Granada	1938-1946
Mardi Gras	1938-1946
Pinecone	1938
Sueno: including Calla Lily, Tulip, Thistle, Pinecone	1938
Orchid	1939-1941
Iris	1940-1942
Leeds: novelty elephant & pig bottles (also converted to lamps)	1940-1944
Morning Glory	1940
Dogwood: a.k.a. Wild Rose	1942-1943
Poppy	1942-1943
Wild Flower Number Series	1942-1943
Classic	1942-1945
Open Rose: a.k.a. Camellia	1943-1944

Magnolia Matte	1946-1947
Wildflower "W" Series	1946-1947
Rosella	1946
Magnolia Gloss	1947-1948
Sunglow: a.k.a. Pansy or Pansy and Butterfly	1948-1949
Water Lily	1948-1949
Bow-Knot	1949-1950
Woodland, (matte finish)	1949-1950
Water Lily, New Gloss	1949-1950
Woodland, New Matte	1950
Woodland, Hi-Gloss	1952-1954
Woodland, Two-Tone	1952-1954
Parchment and Pine	1951-1954
Ebb Tide	1954-1955
Blossom Flite	1955-1956
Butterfly	1956
Serenade	1957
Tokay	1958-1960
Tuscany	1958-1960
Tropicana	1959
Continental	1959-1960

During the war years of the 1940s, Hull Pottery profited when the flow of ceramics from foreign shores was vastly diminished. Hull helped to fill the gaps left by the missing imports on retail store shelves across the country. The company not only provided a vast selection of artwares embellished with peaceful floral sprays or single blooms decorated in soothing pastel glazes, but large quantities of kitchenwares as well. (Roberts 1980, pp. 19-23; Roberts 1992, pp. 68-78)

The artware photographs that follow have been placed in alphabetical order by line name for the convenience of the readers. While not chronologically accurate (as is the above listing), it is hoped this arrangement will make specific patterns easier to find.

Blossom Flite, 1955-1956. Handled basket, T-9, 10" across x 5" high; boat flower bowl, T-12, 10.5" long; and honey jug, T-1, 6" high. *Courtesy of the Collection of Betty and Joe Yonis.* T-9, $140-155; T-12, $100-110; T-1, $60-70

Blossom Flite, 1955-1956.
Back: pitcher, T13, 12.5" high; vase, T7, 9.5" high.
Front: console bowl, T10, 16.5" long x 6.75" high;
candleholder, T11, 3.25" high. *Courtesy of the Collection of
Betty and Joe Yonis.* T13, $220-240; T7, $100-110; T10,
$135-150; T11, $80-90

Blossom Flite, 1955-1956.
Baskets, left to right: T4, 8.5"high and T8, 9.25" diameter.
Courtesy of the Collection of Betty and Joe Yonis. T4, $130-
145; T8, $135-150

Blossom Flite, 1955-1956.
Sugar, T16, teapot, T14, and creamer, T15. The teapot measures
8" high. *Courtesy of the Collection of Betty and Joe Yonis.* T16,
$55-60; T14, $110-120; T15, $55-60

Blossom Flite, 1955-1956.
Boat flower holder, T12, 10.5" long and basket, T2, 6" high.
Courtesy of the Collection of Betty and Joe Yonis. T12, $100-110;
T2, $70-80

Left:
Blossom Flite, 1955-1956.
Interesting variation of the decoration on this
Blossom Flite honey jug, T1, 6" high. *Courtesy of
the Collection of Betty and Joe Yonis.* T1, $65-
75

Below:
Bow-Knot, 1949-1950.
Vase, B-4, 6.5" high; vase, B-2, 5" high; ewer, B-1, 5.5" high;
jardiniere, B-18, 5.75" high; vase, B-3, 6.5" high. *Courtesy of
Michael and Sharon Reinheimer.* B-4, $225-245; B-2, $150-165;
B-1, $160-175; B-18, $225-245; B-3, $225-245

Bow-Knot, 1949-1950.
Top: basket, B-12, 10.5"; vase, B-3, 6.5"; vase, B-4, 6.5".
Bottom: console bowl, B-16, 13.5"; vase, B-2, 5". *Courtesy of the Collection of Betty and Joe Yonis.* B-12, $750-825; B-3, $250-275; B-4, $250-275; B-16, $325-360; B-2, $175-190

Bow-Knot, 1949-1950.
Top: vase, B8, 8.5" high; cornucopia, B5, 7.5" high.
Bottom: vase, B9, 8.5" high; wisk broom wall planter, B27, 8.5" high; wall pocket iron, 4.25" high. *Courtesy of Michael and Sharon Reinheimer.* Top: B8, $245-270; B5, $200-220. Bottom: B9, $245-270; B27 & iron, $300-330 each.

Bow-Knot, 1949-1950.
Left to right: jardiniere, B-19, 9.75"; basket, B-25, 6.5"; planter and saucer, B-6, 6.5"; and iron wall pocket, unmarked (no item number), 6.5". *Courtesy of the Collection of Betty and Joe Yonis.* B-19, $950-1045; B-25, $300-330; B-6, $250-275; wall pocket, $300-330

Bow-Knot, 1949-1950.
Two vases, B-7, 8.5" high. *Courtesy of Michael and Sharon Reinheimer.* $250-275 each

Bow-Knot, 1949-1950.
Two vases, B-14, 12.5" high each. *Courtesy of the Collection of Betty and Joe Yonis.* $1200-1320 each

Bow-Knot, 1949-1950.
Left to right: vases, B-14, 12.5" high and B-11, 10.5" high; basket, B-29, 12" high. *Courtesy of the Collection of Betty and Joe Yonis.* $1200-1320, $500-550, $2000-2200 respectively.

Bow-Knot, 1949-1950.
Creamer, B-21, 4" high; teapot, B-20, 6" high; and sugar bowl, B-22, 4" high. *Courtesy of the Collection of Betty and Joe Yonis.* Teapot, $500-550. Cream & sugar, $175-200 each.

Bow-Knot, 1949-1950.
Tea cup and saucer wall pocket, B-24, 6.5" diameter. *Courtesy of Michael and Sharon Reinheimer.* $250-275

Bow-Knot, 1949-1950.
Pitcher wall pocket, B-26, 6" high. *Courtesy of the Collection of Betty and Joe Yonis.* $265-290

Bow-Knot, 1949-1950.
Two plate wall plaques, B-28, 10" diameter. *Courtesy of the Collection of Betty and Joe Yonis.* $1200-1320 each

Bow-Knot, 1949-1950.
Lamp, 10.75" high. *Courtesy of the Collection of Betty and Joe Yonis.* $2500-2750

Butterfly, 1956.
Fruit bowl, B16, and ashtray, B3. Ashtray, 7" long. *Courtesy of Michael and Sharon Reinheimer.* B16, $80-90; B3, $25-30

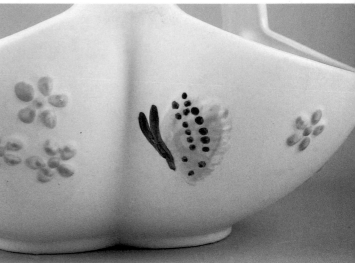

Butterfly, 1956.
Basket, B17, 10.5" high. A different butterfly on each of the three sides. *Courtesy of the Collection of Betty and Joe Yonis.* $325-360

Butterfly, 1956.
Pitcher vase in black with gold trim, B11, 8.75" high.
Courtesy of the Collection of Betty and Joe Yonis. $110-120

Butterfly, 1956.
Pitcher, B15, 13.5" high;
vase, B14, 10.5" high.
*Courtesy of the Collection
of Betty and Joe Yonis.*
B15, $195-215; B14,
$95-105

Butterfly, 1956.
Creamer, B19; sugar, B20; and teapot, B18. Teapot, 8.5" high. *Courtesy of the Collection of Betty and Joe Yonis.* B19, $45-50; B20, $45-50; B18, $170-185

Butterfly, 1956.
Three footed console bowl, B21, 12" diameter. *Courtesy of the Collection of Betty and Joe Yonis.* $170-185

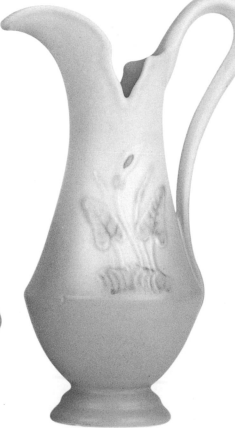

Calla Lily (a.k.a. Jack-in-the-Pulpit), 1938-1940.
Bowl, 500/32, 8" diameter; ewer, 506, 10" high. *Courtesy of Michael and Sharon Reinheimer.* 500, $100-110; 506, $250-275

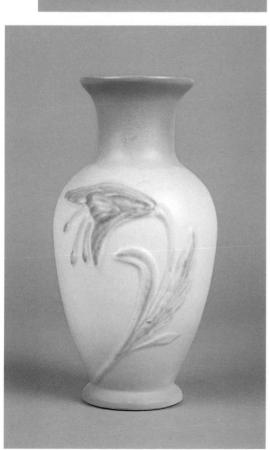

Classic, 1942-1945.
Vase, matte finish, 6.75" high. *Courtesy of the Collection of Betty and Joe Yonis.* $250-275

The new Continental line (1959-1960) was advertised in this catalog as "Sophisticated, Modern Shapes in Three Delightful Decorator Colors" and "Lovely natural colors — accented with rich, bold stripes." The glaze colors were Persimmon, Evergreen, and Mountain Blue. Of these colors, Hull stated: "Persimmon—the completely captivating accent for today's interiors in the higher key of contemporary color;" "Evergreen—a delightfully subtle color that lends itself as a perfect foil to nature's own brilliant floral and leaf displays;" and "Mountain Blue—Imagine twilight in the Blue Mountains—modernized with stripes of white haze."
Courtesy of the Collection of Betty and Joe Yonis.

Lovely natural colors - - -
accented with rich, bold stripes

EVERGREEN --

a delightfully subtle color that lends itself as a perfect foil to nature's own brilliant floral and leaf displays.

Continental - - - beauty that comes from expert craftsmanship, modern designs and finest glazes.

New Continental

Sophisticated, Modern Shapes In Three Delightful Decorator Colors.

MOUNTAIN BLUE — Imagine twilight in the Blue Mountains—modernized with stripes of white haze.

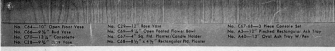

No. C64—10" Open Front Vase No. C29—12" Rose Vase No. C67-68—3 Piece Console Set
No. C66—9½" Bud Vase No. C69—9¼" Open Footed Flower Bowl No. A3—12" Pinched Rectangular Ash Tray
No. C70—13¼" Consolette No. C67—4" Sq. Ftd. Planter/Candle Holder No. A40—13" Oval Ash Tray W/Pen
No. C28—9¾" Vase No. C68—8½" x 4½" Rectangular Ftd. Planter

Hull Pottery Company - - Crooksville, Ohio

Continental

PERSIMMON --

the completely captivating accent for today's interiors in the higher key of contemporary color.

Hull Pottery Company - - Crooksville, Ohio

Continental, 1959-1960.
Free Form vases in the three Continental glaze colors:
Evergreen, Mountain Blue, and Persimmon, C54, 12.5" high.
The Tropicana line used the Continental forms with a white
background glazing and somewhat abstract islander figures
playing musical instruments (largely drums), swimming,
strolling with a rooster and cane, and standing with a staff.
The male figures all wear hats and women have scraves tied
around their heads. These islanders are dressed in pastel
colored outfits. *Courtesy of Michael and Sharon Reinheimer.*
C54, $60-70 each

Continental, 1959-1960.
Vase, C53, 8.5" high. *Courtesy of Thomas F. and
Heather A. Evans.* $50-60

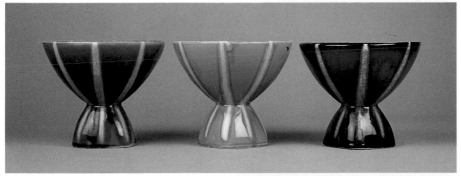

Above and right:
Continental, 1959-1960.
Footed compotes or planters,
C62, 5.5" high x 6.75" diameter.
With a cover, this item became a
candy dish with cover, C62C,
measuring 8.5" high. *Courtesy of
Michael and Sharon Reinheimer.*
C62, $35-40

Continental, 1959-1960.
Pitcher vases, C56, 12.5" high. *Courtesy of Michael and Sharon Reinheimer.* $120-130

Continental, 1959-1960.
Open front vases, C57, 14.5" high. *Courtesy of Michael and Sharon Reinheimer.* $115-125 each (add $10-15 for Mountain Blue glazing)

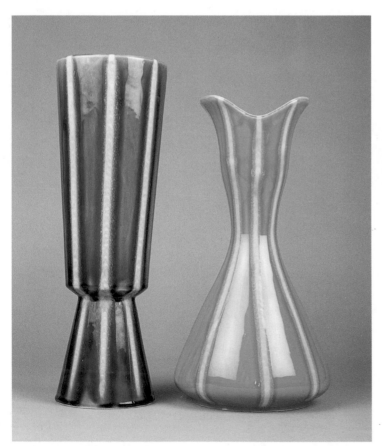

Continental, 1959-1960.
Pedestal vase, C60, 15" high; vase, C58, 13.75" high. *Courtesy of Michael and Sharon Reinheimer.* C60, $125-135; C58, $80-90

Continental, 1959-1960.
Left: Two purpose vase (either a vase or —when overturned— a candleholder), C61, 10" high; center: rose vase, C28, 9.75" high; right: open front vase, C64, 10" high. *Courtesy of Michael and Sharon Reinheimer.* C61, $50-55; C28, $50-55; C64, $60-70

Continental, 1959-1960.
Slender neck vase, C59, 15" high; Rose vase, C29, 12" high; bud vase, C66, 9.5" high. *Courtesy of Thomas F. and Heather A. Evans.* C59, $85-95; C29, $50-55; C66, $45-50

Continental, 1959-1960.
Basket, C55, 12.75" high; consolette, C70, 13.25" long. *Courtesy of Michael and Sharon Reinheimer.* C55, $120-130; C70, $50-55

Continental, 1959-1960.
Basket, C55, 12.75" high. *Courtesy of the Collection of Betty and Joe Yonis.* $120-130

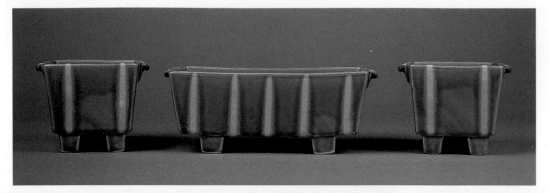

Continental, 1959-1960.
Left and right: square footed planter/candle holder, C67, 4" high; center: rectangular footed planter, C68, 8.5" x 4.5". *Courtesy of Michael and Sharon Reinheimer.* C67, $20-25 each; C68, $25-30

Continental, 1959-1960.
Caladium Leaf (in Persimmon), C63, 14" x 10.5"; ash tray (in Persimmon), A4; ash tray (in Evergreen), C52, 10" x 7.5". *Courtesy of Thomas F. and Heather A. Evans.* C63, $65-75; A4, $65-75; C52, $45-50

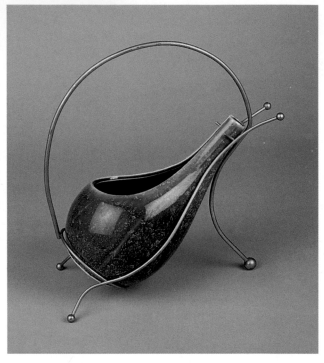

Continental, 1959-1960.
Metal holder and a Continental open front vase, C64, 10" high, holder 12.5" high. *Courtesy of Thomas F. and Heather A. Evans.* $35-40

Crab Apple, 1934-1935.
Vase, (no item numbers), 5" high; jardiniere, 3" high. *Courtesy of Michael and Sharon Reinheimer.* Left: $50-55; Right: $40-45

Dogwood, 1942-1943.
Top: vase, 509, 6.5" high; window box, 508, 10.5" long; vase, 516, 4.75" high.
Bottom: candleholder, 512, 4" high; two cornucopias, 522, 4" high; vase, 517, 4.75" high. *Courtesy of Michael and Sharon Reinheimer.* Top: 509, $115-125; 508, $175-190; 516, $65-76. Bottom: 512, $75-85; 522, $65-75; 517, $65-75

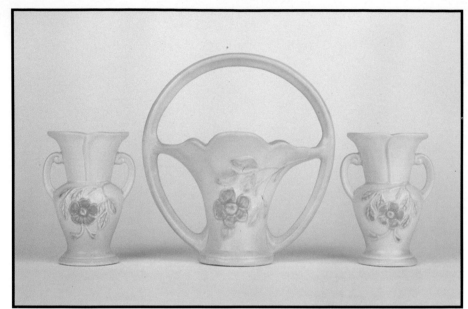

Dogwood, 1942-1943.
Vase, 517, 4.75" high; vase, 501, 7.5" high;
vase, 517, 4.75" high. *Courtesy of Michael and
Sharon Reinheimer.* 517, $65-75; 501, $300-
330; 517, $65-75

Below:
Dogwood, 1942-1943.
Vase, 504, 8.5" high; vase, 513, 6.5" high.
Courtesy of Michael and Sharon Reinheimer.
504, $130-145; 513, $110-120

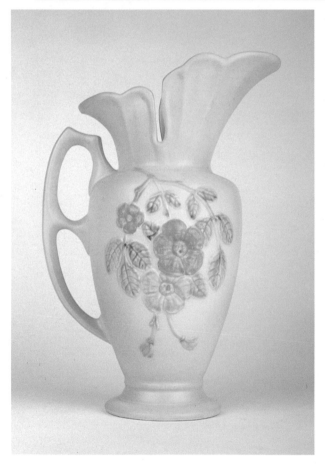

Dogwood, 1942-1943.
Ewer, 519, 13.5" high. *Courtesy of Michael and
Sharon Reinheimer.* $725-795

Right:
Dogwood, 1942-1943.
Hanging basket. Very rare. 8" diameter x 5" high.
Courtesy of the Collection of Betty and Joe Yonis.
$2000-2200

Ebb Tide, "Chartreuse and Wine," 1954-1955 Back: vase, E-1, 7" high; twin fish vase, E-2, 7" high; cornucopia with mermaid, E-3, 7.5" high.
Front: pitcher vases (left & right), E-4, 8.25" high; basket, E-5, 9.25" high. *Courtesy of Michael and Sharon Reinheimer.* Back: E-1, $60-70; E-2, $85-95; E-3, $200-220. Front: E-4, $135-150; E-5, $110-120

Ebb Tide, "Chartreuse and Wine," 1954-1955.
Angel fish vase, E-6, 9.25" high; fish vase, E-7, 11" high; ashtray with mermaid, E-8. *Courtesy of Michael and Sharon Reinheimer.* E-6, $135-150; E-7, $150-165; E-8, $215-235

Ebb Tide, "Chartreuse and Wine," 1954-1955.
Cornucopia, E-9, 11.75" high; pitcher, E-10, 13" high; basket, E-11, 16.5" high. *Courtesy of Michael and Sharon Reinheimer.* E-9, $215-235; E-10, $235-260; E-11, $265-290

Ebb Tide, "Chartreuse and Wine," 1954-1955. Console bowl (with snails), E-12, 15.75"; teapot, E-14; sugar, E-16 (the creamer is E-15); candleholders, E-13. *Courtesy of Michael and Sharon Reinheimer.* E-12, $185-205; E-14, $200-220; E-16 & E-15, $60-70 each; E-13, $85-95

Ebb Tide, "Chartreuse and Wine," 1954-1955. Creamer, E-15; sugar, E-16. *Courtesy of Michael and Sharon Reinheimer.* $60-70 each

Ebb Tide, "Chartreuse and Wine," 1954-1955. Unusual Ebb Tide pieces, employee produced. Left: the base of pitcher, E-10, 8.5" long; center: candleholder; right: the base of console bowl, E-12, 10" long. *Courtesy of Thomas F. and Heather A. Evans.* $55-60 each

Ebb Tide, "Shrimp and Turquoise," 1954-1955. Back: vase, E-1, 7" high; twin fish vase, E-2, 7" high; cornucopia with mermaid, E-3, 7.5" high. Front: pitcher vase, E-4, 8.25" high; basket, E-5, 9.25" high; angel fish vase, E-6, 9.25" high. *Courtesy of Michael and Sharon Reinheimer.* Back: E-1, $60-70; E-2, $85-95; E-3, $200-220. Front: E-4, $135-150; E-5, $110-120; E-6, $135-150

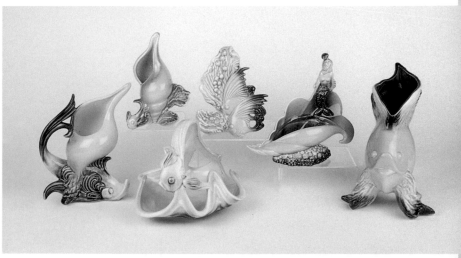

Ebb Tide, "Shrimp and Tur-
quoise," 1954-1955.
Fish vase, E-7, 11" high; ashtray
with mermaid, E-8; cornucopia,
E-9, 11.75" high. *Courtesy of
Michael and Sharon Reinheimer.*
E-7, $150-165; E-8, $215-235;
E-9, $215-235

Ebb Tide, "Shrimp and Turquoise," 1954-1955.
Pitcher, E-10, 13" high; basket, E-11, 16.5" high.
Courtesy of Michael and Sharon Reinheimer. E-10,
$235-260; E-11, $265-290

Ebb Tide, "Shrimp and Turquoise,"
1954-1955.
Candleholders, E-13; console bowl
(with snails), E-12, 15.75"; teapot, E-14;
creamer, E-15; sugar, E-16. *Courtesy of
Michael and Sharon Reinheimer.* E-13,
$85-95; E-12, $185-205; E-14, $200-
220; E-15, $60-70; E-16, $60-70

Granada/Mardis Gras, 1938-1946; Morning Glory, 1940.
Left and right: Mardi Gras/Granada (vases from this line are not ususally decorated to this degree), 66, 10" high.
Center: Morning Glory, 63, 11" high. *Courtesy of Michael and Sharon Reinheimer.* 66, $175-190 each; 63, $400-440

Ebb Tide, 1954-1955.
An odd sample piece—an Ebb Tide shape in Woodland glaze colors. *Courtesy of the Collection of Betty and Joe Yonis.* $250-275

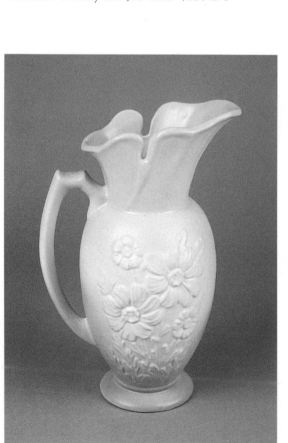

Granada/Mardis Gras, 1938-1946.
Basket, 65, 8" high. *Courtesy of the Collection of Betty and Joe Yonis.* $160-175

Granada/Mardis Gras, 1938-1946.
Pitcher, 31, 10.25" high. *Courtesy of the Collection of Betty and Joe Yonis.* $120-130

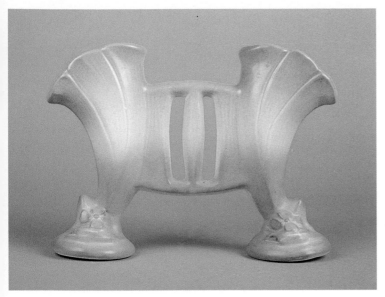

Granada/Mardi Gras, 1938-1946.
Rare double bud vase, 6" high x 8" long. *Courtesy of the Collection of Betty and Joe Yonis.* $500-550

Iris, 1940-1942.
Vase, 414, 10.5" high; two vases, 407, 4.75" high.
Courtesy of Michael and Sharon Reinheimer.
414, $400-440; 407, $75-85

Iris, 1940-1942.
Ewer, 401, 13.5" high. Here is a close look at the pattern. *Courtesy of Michael and Sharon Reinheimer.* $400-440

Iris, 1940-1942.
Vase, 406, 7" high; vase, 403, 7" high; ewer, 401, 8" high; vase, 405, 7" high. *Courtesy of Michael and Sharon Reinheimer.* 406, $125-135; 403, $130-140; 401, $235-260; 405, $125-135

Iris, 1940-1942.
Vase, 403, 8.5" high; vase, 405, 8.5" high; vase, 402, 7" high. *Courtesy of Michael and Sharon Reinheimer.* 403, $160-175; 405, $160-175; 402, $120-130

Below:
Iris, 1940-1942.
Vase, 414, 16" high; vase, 414, 10.5" high; console bowl, 409, 12" long. *Courtesy of Michael and Sharon Reinheimer.* 414, $550-605; 414, $350-385; 409, $200-220

Leeds, 1940-1944.
Elephant liquor bottle converted into a lamp. Elephant, 7" high. *Courtesy of the Collection of Betty and Joe Yonis.* $125-135

Leeds.
Elephant and pig liquor bottles, 7.5" high. *Courtesy of Michael and Sharon Reinheimer.* $50-55 each

Magnolia Gloss, 1947-1948.
Vase, H-8, 8.5" high. *Courtesy of the Collection of Betty and Joe Yonis.* $75-85

Below:
Water Lily, 1948-1949, and **Magnolia Gloss, 1947-1948.**
Left: Matte with gold gilt Water Lily cornucopia, L-7, 6.5" high.
Right: Magnolia Gloss (1947-1948) vase, H-5, 6.5" high. *Courtesy of the Collection of Betty and Joe Yonis.* L-7, $100-110; H-5, $40-45

Below:
Magnolia Gloss, 1947-1948.
Sugar, H-22, 3.75" high; teapot, H-20, 6.5" high; creamer, H-21, 3.75" high. *Courtesy of the Collection of Betty and Joe Yonis.* H-22 & H-21, $55-60 each; H-20, $185-200

Magnolia Matte, 1946-1947.
Vases, 2, 8.5" high. *Courtesy of Michael and Sharon Reinheimer.* $110-120

Magnolia Matte, 1946-1947.
Left to right: vase, 7, 8.5" high; vase, 1, 8.5" high; vase, 1, 8.5" high. *Courtesy of Michael and Sharon Reinheimer.* Left to right: #7, $125-135; #1, $110-120 each.

Magnolia Matte, 1946-1947.
Vases and pitcher. Vase, 11, 6.5" high; vase, 12, 6.5" high; vase, 4, 6.5" high; pitcher, 5, 7" high. *Courtesy of Michael and Sharon Reinheimer.* #11, $50-55; #12, $50-55; #4, $50-55; #5, $115-125

Magnolia Matte, 1946-1947.
Top: basket, 10, 10.5" high; vase, 3, 8.5" high. Bottom: teapot, 23, 6.5" high; sugar, 25, 3.75" high; creamer, 24. Note: the lid on the sugar bowl may not be correct. *Courtesy of Michael and Sharon Reinheimer.* Top: 10, $300-330; 3, $100-110. Bottom: 23, $215-235; 25 & 24, $75-85 each

Magnolia Matte, 1946-1947.
Left to right: cornucopia, 19, 8.5" high; double cornucopia, 6, 12" long; cornucopia, 19, 8.5" high. *Courtesy of Michael and Sharon Reinheimer.* #19, $100-110 each; #6, $165-180

Magnolia Matte, 1946-1947.
Vases (loop handles), 15, 6.25" high. *Courtesy of Michael and Sharon Reinheimer.* $50-55

Magnolia Matte, 1946-1947.
Small vases and pitchers. Left: vases, 13, 4.75" high. Right: pitchers, 14, 4.75" high. *Courtesy of Michael and Sharon Reinheimer.* #13, $40-45; #14, $50-55

Magnolia Matte, 1946-1947.
Ewer, 18, 13.5" high; vase, 9, 10.5" high; vase, 8, 10.5" high. *Courtesy of Michael and Sharon Reinheimer.* 18, $325-355; 9, $160-175; 8, $140-155

Magnolia Matte, 1946-1947.
Vase, 22, 12.5" high; console bowl, 26, 12.5" long. *Courtesy of Michael and Sharon Reinheimer.* 22, $275-300; 26, $150-165

Magnolia Matte, 1946-1947.
Vase, 20, 15" high; ewer, 18, 13.5" high; vase, 17, 12.25" high. *Courtesy of Michael and Sharon Reinheimer.* 20, $450-495; 18, $325-355; 17, $285-310

Magnolia Matte, 1946-1947. Tassel vases, 21, 12.5" high. Note the open or closed loops in the tassels. *Courtesy of Michael and Sharon Reinheimer.* $285-315 each

Morning Glory, 1940.
Vase, 8.75" high. The Morning Glory pattern was developed but never put into mass-production, making wares decorated in the Morning Glory motif very rare finds indeed. *Courtesy of the Collection of Betty and Joe Yonis.* $500-550

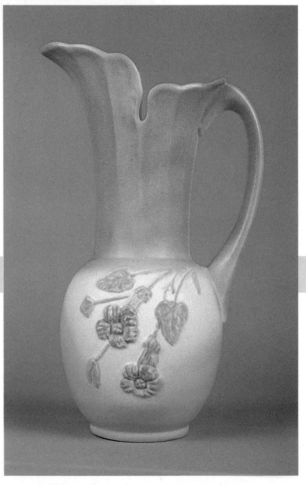

Morning Glory, 1940.
Pitcher vase, long necked, 11" high. Rarely seen. *Courtesy of the Collection of Betty and Joe Yonis.* $1200-1320

Open Rose (a.k.a. Camellia), 1943-1944.
Vase, 102, 8.5" high; vase, 103, 8.5" high; cornucopia, 101, 8.5" high. *Courtesy of Michael and Sharon Reinheimer.* 102, $140-155; 103, $150-165; 101, $125-135

Open Rose (a.k.a. Camellia), 1943-1944.
Ewer, 105, 7" high; basket, 107, 8" high; vase, 119, 8.5" high. *Courtesy of Michael and Sharon Reinheimer.* 105, $200-220; 107, $300-330; 119, $165-180

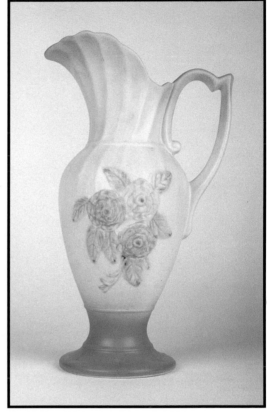

Open Rose (a.k.a. Camellia), 1943-1944.
Ewer, 106, 13.25" high. *Courtesy of Michael and Sharon Reinheimer.* $550-605

Open Rose (a.k.a. Camellia), 1943-1944.
Vase, 126, 8.5" high; vase, 141, 8.5" high; vase, 108, 8.5" high. *Courtesy of Michael and Sharon Reinheimer.* 126, $285-315; 141, $150-165; 108, $175-190

Open Rose (a.k.a. Camellia), 1943-1944.
Teapot, lid missing, 110, 8.5" high. *Courtesy of the Collection of Betty and Joe Yonis.* $360-395 (complete)

Open Rose (a.k.a. Camellia), 1943-1944.
Low bowl (note the ram's head handles), 113, 7"; vases, 138, 6.25" high.
Courtesy of Michael and Sharon Reinheimer. 113, $115-125; 138, $135-150

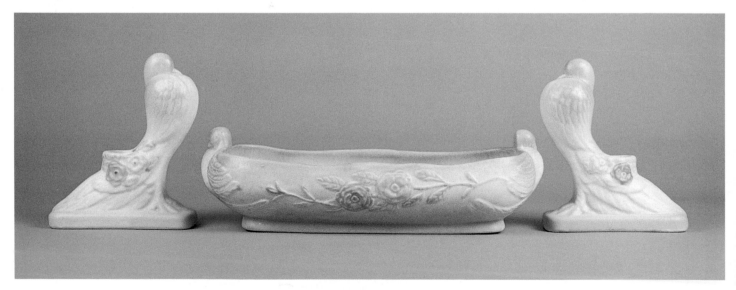

Open Rose (a.k.a. Camellia), 1943-1944.
Dove console bowl, 116, 12" long and candleholders, 117, 6.5" high. *Courtesy of the Collection of Betty and Joe Yonis.* 116, $335-370; 117, $300-330 pair

Open Rose (a.k.a. Camellia), 1943-1944.
Back: vase, 120, 6.25" high; vase, 121, 6.25" high.
Front: vases, 118, 6.5 high. *Courtesy of Michael and Sharon Reinheimer.* Back: 120, $125-135; 121, $125-135. Front: 118, $135-150

Open Rose (a.k.a. Camellia), 1943-1944.
Vases and small pitcher.
Back: vase, 122, 6.25; vase, 123, 6.25:
Front: vase 130, 4.75" high; ewer, 128, 4.75" high. *Courtesy of Michael and Sharon Reinheimer.* Back: 122, $125-135; 123, $125-135. Front: 130, $75-85; 128, $75-85

Open Rose (a.k.a. Camellia), 1943-1944.
Bud vase, 129, 7" high; vase, 127, 4.75" high, vase, 131, 4.75"high. *Courtesy of Michael and Sharon Reinheimer.* 129, $125-135; 127, $75-85; 131, $75-85

Open Rose (a.k.a. Camellia), 1943-1944.
Vase, 135, 6.25" high; vase, 136, 6.25" high; vase,
137, 6.25" high. *Courtesy of Michael and Sharon
Reinheimer.* 135, $135-150; 136, $135-150; 137,
$135-150

Orchid, 1939-1941.
Back: candleholders, 315.
Front: vase, 308, 4.75" high;
vase, 303, 4.75" high;
jardiniere, 310, 6" high;
vase, 307, 4.75" high; vase,
302, 4.75" high. *Courtesy of
Michael and Sharon
Reinheimer.* Back: 315,
$215-235. Front: 308, $85-
95; 303, $75-85; 310,
$200-220; 307, $100-110;
302, $75-85

Orchid, 1939-1941.
Basket, 305. The handle broke off during production in the factory and workers smoothed down the breaks and glazed them over to make this unique piece. Shown with the complete vase. 4.75" high without handle. 7" high with handle. *Courtesy of the Collection of Betty and Joe Yonis.* Handleless, $400-440; with handle, $550-600.

Orchid, 1939-1941.
Lamp, 10.75" high. *Courtesy of the Collection of Betty and Joe Yonis.* $750-825

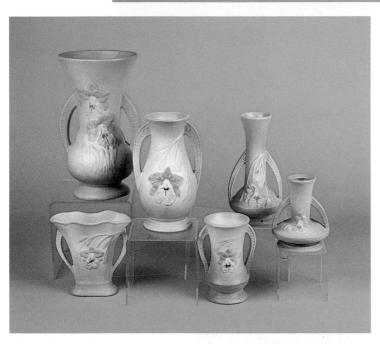

Orchid, 1939-1941.
Vases and candleholders.
Back: vase, 301, 10" high; vase, 302, 8" high; bud vase, 306, 6.75" high; candleholder, 315, 4" high.
Front: vase, 307, 6.5" high; vase, 308, 6.5" high. *Courtesy of the Collection of Betty and Joe Yonis.* Back: 301, $330-360; 302, $200-220; 306, $150-165; 315, 230-255 pair. Front: 307, $150-165; 308, $150-165.

Orchid, 1939-1941.
Large console bowl, 314, 13" handle to handle. *Courtesy of the Collection of Betty and Joe Yonis.* $400-440

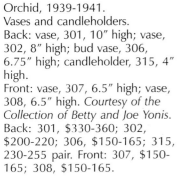

Orchid, 1939-1941.
Lamps, 7.25" high. *Courtesy of the Collection of Betty and Joe Yonis.*
$1500-1650 each

Orchid, 1939-1941.
Two lamps, 9.75" high. *Courtesy of the Collection of Betty and Joe Yonis.* $650-715 each

Parchment and Pine, 1951-1954.
Bud vase, S-1, 6.75" high. *Courtesy of Michael and Sharon Reinheimer.* $35-40

Parchment and Pine, 1951-1954.
Pitcher, S-7, 13.5" high. *Courtesy of the Collection of Betty and Joe Yonis.* $220-240

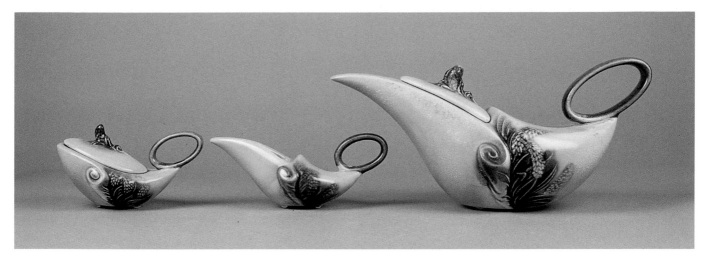

Parchment and Pine, 1951-1954.
Sugar, S-13, 3.25" high; creamer, S-12, 3.25" high; teapot, S-11, 6" high. *Courtesy of the Collection of Betty and Joe Yonis.* S-12 & S-13, $40-45 each; S-11, $130-145

Parchment and Pine, 1951-1954.
Console bowl, S-9, 16" long. *Courtesy of Michael and Sharon Reinheimer.* $60-70

Poppy, 1942-1943.
Vase (signed with a Z initial), 607, 10.5" high; vase, 607, 8.5" high; leaf vase (signed with an M initial), 604, 8" long. *Courtesy of Michael and Sharon Reinheimer.* 607, $425-465; 607, $225-245, 604, $300-330

Poppy, 1942-1943.
Vase, 605, 8.5" high; leaf vase, 604, 8" long; vase, 608, 4.75" high. *Courtesy of Michael and Sharon Reinheimer.* 605, $225-250; 604, $300-330; 608, $135-150

Poppy, 1942-1943.
Vase, 612, 6.5" high; vase, 611, 6.5" high; jardiniere, 608, 4.75" high; ewer, 610, 4.25" high. *Courtesy of Michael and Sharon Reinheimer.* 612, $175-190; 611, $175-190; 608, $135-150; 610, $135-150

Rosella, 1946.
Top: vase, R-15, 8.5" high; ewer, R-11, 7" high; vase, R-8, 6" high; vase, R-7, 6.5" high.
Bottom: basket, R-12, 7" high; vase, R-1, 5" high; sugar bowl, R-4, 5.5"high; Creamer, R-3, 5.5" high. *Courtesy of Michael and Sharon Reinheimer.* Top: R-15, $60-70; R-11, $60-70; R-8, $65-75; R-7, $40-45. Bottom: R-12, $150-165; R-1, $25-30; R-4, $45-50; R-3, $45-50

Rosella, 1946.
Three wall pockets. Left: Athena wall pocket, 611. Center: Chinese Sage Mask wall pocket, 120. Right: **Rosella** heart-shaped wall pocket (1946), marked Hull Art, R-10, 6.5". *Courtesy of the Collection of Betty and Joe Yonis.* 611, $130-145; 120, $100-110; Rosella, $90-100

Rosella, 1946.
Lamp, 6" high. *Courtesy of the Collection of Betty and Joe Yonis.* $125-135

Serenade, 1957.
Pitcher, S8, 8.5" high; teapot, S17, 6 cup; and pitcher, S2, 6" high. Note: on the pitcher to the left is shown a single bird on the back of the piece. *Courtesy of the Collection of Betty and Joe Yonis.* S8, $90-100; S17, $170-185; S2, $65-75

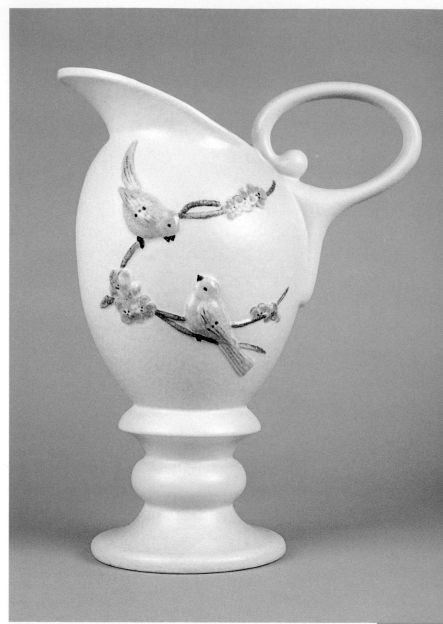

Serenade, 1957.
Pitcher, S13, 13.5" high. *Courtesy of the Collection of Betty and Joe Yonis.* $370-400

Serenade, 1957.
Basket, S14, 12" high. *Courtesy of the Collection of Betty and Joe Yonis.* $340-375

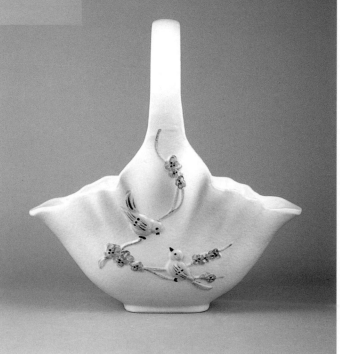

Serenade, 1957.
Sugar bowl, S19, 3.5" high. *Courtesy of the Collection of Betty and Joe Yonis.* $50-55

Sunglow, 1948-1949.
Vase, 92, 6.5" high; bowl, 50, 7.5" diameter; bell, 6" high;
pitcher, 52, 24 oz.; salt and pepper shakers, 54, 2.75" high.
Courtesy of the Collection of Betty and Joe Yonis. 92, $45-50;
50, $35-40; bell, $185-200; 52, $40-45; 54, $20-25

Sunglow, 1948-1949.
Three bells. Two with loop handles and one with a solid handle.
Courtesy of the Collection of Betty and Joe Yonis. Loop
handled, $220-240; solid handled, $185-200

Sunglow, 1948-1949.
Unique colors on this Sunglow pitcher wall pocket,
81, 5.25" high. *Courtesy of the Collection of Betty and
Joe Yonis.* $200-220

Tulip (Sueno), 1938-1941.
Vase, 101-33, 9" high. *Courtesy of Michael and Sharon Reinheimer.* $220-240

Tulip (Sueno), 1938-1941.
Top: vase, 100-33, 8" high; vase, 105-33, 8" high; vase, 111-33, 6" high; vase, 103-33, 6" high.
Bottom: basket, 102-33, 6" high; vase, 100-33, 6.5" high; vase, 110-33, 6" high; jardiniere, 117-30, 5" high. *Courtesy of Michael and Sharon Reinheimer.* Top: 100-33, $200-220; 105-33, $200-220; 111-33, $135-150; 103-33, $235-260. Bottom: 102-33, $275-300; 100-33, $110-120; 110-33, $125-135; 117-30, $100-110

Tulip (Sueno), 1938-1941.
Vase, 108-33, 6" high; vase, 106-33, 6" high; bud vase, 104-44, 6" high. *Courtesy of Michael and Sharon Reinheimer.* 108, $125-135; 106, $125-135; 104, $125-135

Tulip (Sueno), 1938-1941.
Lamp, 8.5" high. *Courtesy of the Collection of Betty and Joe Yonis.* $750-825

Water Lily, 1948-1949. Back: vase, L-9, 8.5" high; double cornucopia, L-27, 12" high; jardiniere, L-24, 8.5" high; vase, L-1, 5.5" high. Front: cornucopia, L-7, 6.5" high; ewer, L-3, 5.5" high; candleholder, L-22; vase, L-2, 5.5" high; candleholder, L-22. *Courtesy of Michael and Sharon Reinheimer.* Back: L-9, $185-205; L-27, $230-255; L-24, $320-350; L-1, $55-60. Front: L-7, $85-95; L-3, $80-90; L-22, $110-120 pair; L-2, $55-60

Water Lily, 1948-1949. Teapots, creamers and sugars in two glaze treatments. Teapot, L-18, 6" high; creamer, L-19, 5" high; sugar, L-20, 5" high. *Courtesy of Michael and Sharon Reinheimer.* L-18, $215-235; L-19 & L-20, $75-85 each

Water Lily, 1948-1949.
Left to right: vase, L-12, 10.5" high; vase, L-13, 10.5" high; vase, L-10, 9.5" high. *Courtesy of Michael and Sharon Reinheimer.* L-12, $235-260; L-13, $235-260; L-10, $175-190

Water Lily, 1948-1949.
Basket, L-14, 10.5" high; vase, L-13, 10.5" high; vase, L-A, 8.5" high; ewer, L-17, 13.5" high. *Courtesy of Michael and Sharon Reinheimer.* L-14, $325-355; L-13, $225-245; L-A, $150-165; L-17, $400-440

Water Lily, 1948-1949.
Vase, L-8, 8.5" high; vase, L-5, 6.5" high; vase, L-6, 6.5" high. *Courtesy of Michael and Sharon Reinheimer.* L-8, $100-110; L-5, $85-95; L-6, $85-95

Water Lily, 1948-1949.
Left to right: vase, L-16, 12.5" high;
vase, L-4, 6.5" high. *Courtesy of Michael
and Sharon Reinheimer.* L-16, $375-
410; L-4, $75-85

Below:
Water Lily, 1948-1949.
Lamp, 7.75" high. *Courtesy of the
Collection of Betty and Joe Yonis.*
$2200-2420

Water Lily, 1948-1949.
Unusual glaze colors on a Water Lily cornucopia, L-7, 6.5" high.
Courtesy of the Collection of Betty and Joe Yonis. $200-220

Wildflower Number Series, 1942-1943.
Vase, 77, 10.5" high; vase, 59, 10.5" high; vase, 67, 8.5" high. *Courtesy of Michael and Sharon Reinheimer.* 77, $375-410; 59, $335-370; 67, $300-330

Wildflower Number Series, 1942-1943.
Vase, 52, 6.25" high; vase, 62, 6.25" high. *Courtesy of Michael and Sharon Reinheimer.* 52, $140-155; 62, $150-165

Bottom two photos:
Wildflower Number Series, 1942-1943.
Basket, 66, 10.25" high. *Courtesy of Michael and Sharon Reinheimer.* $1500-1650

Wildflower Number Series, 1942-1943.
Left and center: basket, 66, 10.25" high (with handle).
Right: basket, 79, 10.25" high. Note the center vase lacks a handle. A unique variation produced this way at the factory, probably salvaging a piece with a broken handle prior to firing. *Courtesy of the Collection of Betty and Joe Yonis.* Left: $1500-1650; center: $2200-2420; right: $1600-1760

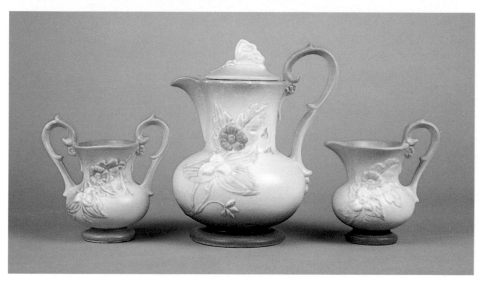

Wildflower Number Series, 1942-1943.
Sugar, teapot, and creamer. Sugar, 74, 4.75" high; teapot, 72, 8.25" high; creamer, 73, 4.75" high. *Courtesy of the Collection of Betty and Joe Yonis.* 73 & 74, $250-275 each; 72, $1200-1320

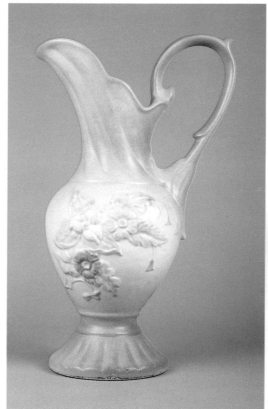

Wildflower Number Series, 1942-1943.
Ewer, 55, 13.5" high. *Courtesy of the Collection of Betty and Joe Yonis.* $1500-1650

Wildflower Number Series, 1942-1943.
Vases, cornucopia, and jardiniere.
Back: vase, 77, 10.5" high; vase, 78, 8.5" high; cornucopia, 58, 6.5".
Front: vase, 59, 10.5" high; vase, 62, 6.5" high; jariniere, 64, 4" high. *Courtesy of the Collection of Betty and Joe Yonis.* Back: 77, $400-440; 78, $400-440; 58, $165-180. Front: 59, $375-410; 62, $175-190; 64, $125-135

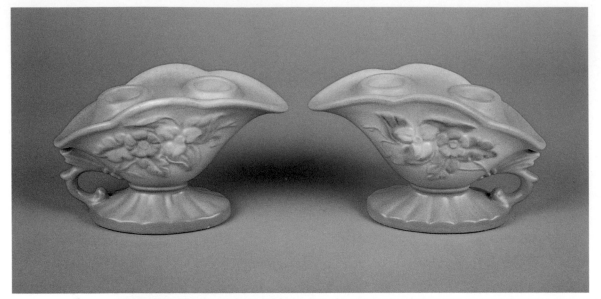

Wildflower Number Series, 1942-1943. Candleholders, 69, 6" long x 4" high. *Courtesy of the Collection of Betty and Joe Yonis.* $300-330 pair

Wildflower "W" Series, 1946-1947.
Top: vase signed with a Z for the designer Zelda, W12, 9.5" high; vase, W9, 8.5" high; pitcher, W11, 8.5" high; pitcher, W11, 8.5" high.
Bottom: cornucopias, W7, 8.5" high. *Courtesy of Michael and Sharon Reinheimer.* Top: W12, $150-165; W9, $135-150; W11, $150-165 each. Bottom: W7, $85-95

Wildflower "W" Series, 1946-1947.
Top: vase, W8, 7.5" high; vase, W4, 6.5" high; vase, W4, 6.5" high.
Bottom: vase, W5, 6.5" high; vase (with an incised "A"), W3, 5.5" high. *Courtesy of Michael and Sharon Reinheimer.* Top: W8, $80-90; W4, $70-80 each. Bottom: W5, $75-85; W3, $50-55

Wildflower "W" Series, 1946-1947.
Vase, W-15, 10.5" high; vase, W-14, 10.5" high; vase, W-13, 9.5" high. *Courtesy of Michael and Sharon Reinheimer.* W-15, $160-175; W-14, $165-180; W-13, $150-165

Wildflower "W" Series, 1946-1947.
Cornucopia, W-10, 8.5" high; basket, W-16, 10.5" high; ewer, W-2, 5.5" high. *Courtesy of Michael and Sharon Reinheimer.* W-10, $100-110; W-16, $350-385; W-2, $75-85

Wildflower "W" Series, 1946-1947.
Floor vase, W20, 15" high; vase, W5, 6.5" high; vase, W1, 5.5" high. *Courtesy of Michael and Sharon Reinheimer.* W20, $400-440; W5, $70-80; W1, $50-55

Above:
Woodland, 1949-1954 (several glaze variations produced).
Oval console bowl, W29, 14" long; candleholders, W30; vase, W4, 6.5" high. *Courtesy of Michael and Sharon Reinheimer.* W29, $250-275; W30, $50-55 each; W4, $100-110

Right:
Wildflower "W" Series, 1946-1947.
Vase, W17, 12.5" high; vase, W9, 8.5" high. *Courtesy of Michael and Sharon Reinheimer.* W17, $275-300; W9, $130-145

Below:
Woodland, 1949-1954 (several glaze variations produced).
Top: vase, W1, 5.5" high; console bowl, W29, 14" long; vase, W16, 8.5" high.
Center: cornucopia vase, W5, 6.5" high; candleholders, W30, 3.5" high; ewer (pitcher), W3, 5.5" high; window box, W19, 10.5" long.
Bottom: cornucopia, W10, 11" long; shell wall pocket, W13, 7.5" high. *Courtesy of Michael and Sharon Reinheimer.* **Top:** W1, $80-90; W29, $250-275; W16, $150-165. **Center:** W5, $70-80; W30, $50-55; W3, $100-110; W19, $120-130. **Bottom:** W10, $150-165; W13, $170-185

Woodland, 1949-1954 (several glaze variations produced).
Vase, W18, 10.5" high; hanging basket, W12, 7.5" high; jardiniere, W7, 5.5" high. *Courtesy of Michael and Sharon Reinheimer.* W18, $185-205; W12, $500-550; W7, $130-145

Woodland, 1949-1954 (several glaze variations produced).
Top: vase, W17, 7.5" high; vase, W8, 7.5" high.
Bottom: ewer, W6, 5.25" high; basket, W9, 8.25" high; cornucopia, W2, 5.25" high. *Courtesy of Michael and Sharon Reinheimer.* Top: W17, $235-260; W8, $110-120. Bottom: W6, $110-120; W9, $220-240; W2, $75-85

Woodland, 1949-1954 (several glaze variations produced).
Cornucopia, W10, 10". *Courtesy of Michael and Sharon Reinheimer.* $175-190

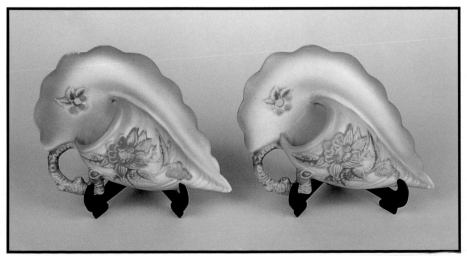

Woodland, 1949-1954 (several glaze variations produced).
Wall Pockets, W13, 7.5" high. *Courtesy of Michael and Sharon Reinheimer.* $170-185

Woodland, 1949-1954 (several glaze variations produced).
Tea set. Teapot, W26, 10.75" long; sugar, W28; creamer, W27. *Courtesy of Michael and Sharon Reinheimer.* W26, $300-330; W28, $75-85; W27, $75-85

Woodland, 1949-1954 (several glaze variations produced).
Ewer in rare colors, W24, 13.5" high. *Courtesy of the Collection of Betty and Joe Yonis.* $750-825

Woodland, 1949-1954 (several glaze variations produced).
Lamp. 14" high. Very rare. *Courtesy of the Collection of Betty and Joe Yonis.* $900-990

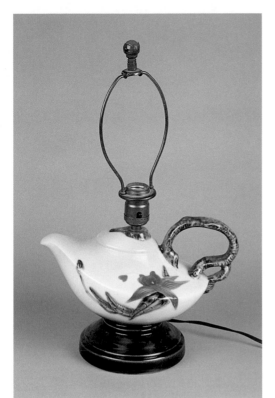

Left:
Woodland, 1949-1954 (several glaze variations produced). Lamp, 8.25" high. *Courtesy of the Collection of Betty and Joe Yonis.* $600-660

Woodland, 1949-1954 (several glaze variations produced). Very rare lamp, 14" high. *Courtesy of the Collection of Betty and Joe Yonis.* $800-880

Woodland, 1949-1954 (several glaze variations produced). Lamp, 14" high. *Courtesy of the Collection of Betty and Joe Yonis.* $500-550

Kitchenwares

In fact, during this period—and throughout the life of Hull Pottery—kitchenwares remained a mainstay of the organization. Decorative motifs and body shapes would be updated regularly to reflect the trends of the passing decades. Early semi-porcelain kitchenwares and related items, in production from 1930 to 1940, included nested bowls, casseroles, cookie jars, custards, jugs, and similar useful items decorated in a variety of underglazed colored bands or with overglazed Mexican decorative motifs. From 1932 to 1935 a line of colorful teapots and covered ovenware was offered. Between 1937 and 1940, Hull offered a Nuline Bak-Serve ovenproof kitchenware line including some eighteen different forms, including a cookie jar. The Bak-Serve line was decorated in three distinct embossed patterns: the Diamond Quilt "B", the Fish Scale "C", and Drape and Panel "D" designs. The Bak-Serve line came glazed in high gloss, solid blue, cream, maroon, peach, turquoise, and yellow.

Nuline Bak-Serve.
Teapot, two covered casseroles and one covered bean pot, lid missing. Teapot, 5, 6" high; covered casseroles, 13, 7.5" diameter; bean pot, 19, 4.5" diameter. *Courtesy of the Collection of Betty and Joe Yonis.* Teapot, $80-90; casseroles, $45-55 each; bean pot (lid missing), $20-25

Nuline Bak-Serve.
Small covered bowl, 4.75" high. *Courtesy of Michael and Sharon Reinheimer.* $20-25

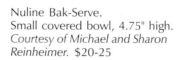

Little Red Riding Hood.
Cookie jars, 13" high. The yellow cast to the center cookie jar indicates it was made at Hull. The other two were made by Royal China and Novelty Company for Hull. Left: decorated in Poinsettia. Salt and pepper shakers are decorated in the same pattern. *Courtesy of Michael and Sharon Reinheimer.* Poinsettia, $1200-1320; Open basket, $375-410; Closed basket, $375-410

During this period, the restaurants and hotels were not forgotten. Lines of plain white semi-porcelain wares suitable for these trades were offered during the 1930s.

At the height of the Second World War, designer Louise E. Bauer of Zanesville patented a novel kitchenware line that struck a chord with war-weary Americans. On June 29, 1943, Louise Bauer patented a cookie jar designed as Little Red Riding Hood. (Figural cookie jars had just come into fashion in the late 1930s.) The patent design was assigned to the A.E. Hull Pottery Company, Inc. This proved to be a popular item, and sold well for the company until 1957, when the initial patent expired. A variety of wares were produced in the Red Riding Hood motif. However, the vast majority of these were sent as undecorated blanks (fired wares ready for glazing and other decorations) to the Royal China and Novelty Company of Chicago, Illinois, for decorations and decals.

Little Red Riding Hood.
Grease jar, 8.5" high. This is one of a few pieces of Little Red Riding Hood actually made by Hull. The rest were contracted out to Royal. *Courtesy of Michael and Sharon Reinheimer.* $750-825

Little Red Riding Hood.
Coffee, tea, and spice containers. Coffee & tea, 9.5" high. All spice & cloves, 5"
high. *Courtesy of Michael and Sharon Reinheimer.* Coffee & tea: $700-770; all
spice, $800-880; cloves, $800-880

Little Red Riding Hood.
Sugar and Cereal containers, 9.5" high. *Courtesy of Michael and*
Sharon Reinheimer. Sugar: $650-715; cereal, $1000-1100

Little Red Riding Hood.
Shakers. 5", 4.5", 3.75" high. *Courtesy of Michael and Sharon Reinheimer.*
Left to right: 5", $165-180; 4.5", $1300-1430; 3.75", $100-110

Little Red Riding Hood.
Shakers showing variation in decoration (decal), 3.75" high.
Courtesy of Michael and Sharon Reinheimer. $100-110

Little Red Riding Hood.
Three cream and sugar sets. Creamers, 4.75" & 5" high. Right creamer figure has pantaloons. *Courtesy of Michael and Sharon Reinheimer.* Left sugar: $300-330; left creamer:
$300-330; center sugar (side pour), $180; center ceramer (side pour), $180; right creamer
(pantaloons), $500-550; right sugar (with lid), $500-550

Little Red Riding Hood.
Wall pocket, match holder and
mustard jar with spoon. Wall pocket,
9.5" high; match holder, 6" high;
mustard jar, 2.25" high; spoon, 4.5"
long. *Courtesy of Michael and
Sharon Reinheimer.* Left: $500-550;
center: $750-825; right: $500-550

Little Red Riding Hood.
Milk pitcher, covered butter, and batter pitcher. Pitcher, 8" high; covered butter, 6.75" long; batter, 6.75" high. *Courtesy of Michael and Sharon Reinheimer.* Left: $400-440; center: $450-495; right: $500-550

Little Red Riding Hood.
Cracker jar and teapot. Jar, 8" high; teapot, 7.75" high. *Courtesy of Michael and Sharon Reinheimer.* Jar: $800-880; teapot, $375-410

Left:
Little Red Riding Hood.
Standing wall bank, 7" high. *Courtesy of Michael and Sharon Reinheimer.* $800-880

Little Red Riding Hood.
Cookie jar and salt & pepper shakers decorated with the Poinsettia pattern. Note the black shoes on this cookie jar. Others had brown or red shoes. *Courtesy of Michael and Sharon Reinheimer.* Cookie jar: $1200-1320

Aside from artwares and kitchenwares, the company also produced lamps based largely on their artware motifs. Fittings could be added to the ceramic lamp bases at the buyer's request. Particularly in the vicinity of Crooksville, Ohio, collectors may find lamps produced and decorated by the employees on their own time and for their own purposes. These unique lamps are highly prized when they are found.

In the summer of 1950, the company suffered from a reversal in fortune brought about by a reversal of an old cliché: "high water and hell." On June 16, a sudden downpour caused local creeks to flood. The flood waters inundated Crooksville, struck the everhot Hull pottery kilns, which exploded, and brought the factory down in flames amidst the flood waters.

Hull Pottery proved to be resilient. Within a week the company was shipping from temporary quarters. By 1952, the plant was remodeled with modern equipment. James Brannon Hull was in charge of the operations and the company name was shortened to the Hull Pottery Company. With new equipment, multiple patterns were produced every year and artwares were produced in abundance. Impressive designs reflecting the contemporary styles of the 1950s were created with both pastel and high gloss glazes. Butterfly, Serenade, and Tokay artware lines all featured pastel glazes while Blossom Flite, the deep sea themed Ebb Tide, and Parchment and Pine sported high gloss glaze coatings. During this period, popular body shapes would appear, with minor variations, in any number of artware lines, both with or without embossed surface decorations.

Kitchenwares were manufactured in vast quantities in the 1950s as well. Many of the 1950s kitchenware lines sported a new glaze treatment, the "foam edge." To create the foam edge, an object's rim was dipped in a second, contrasting glaze coating

Poppy.
Lamp, 9" high. *Courtesy of the Collection of Betty and Joe Yonis.* $700-770

Modern, plaid decoration.
Back: two bowls and cookie jar. Front: sugar bowl, salt and pepper shakers, grease jar (lid missing), and salt and pepper shakers. 9" high cookie jar. *Courtesy of Michael and Sharon Reinheimer.* Back, left to right: $20-25; $15-16; $175-190. Front: sugar, $40-45; salt & pepper, $35-40; grease jar, $60-70; salt & pepper, $35-40

prior to firing. During the glaze firing, the rim coat would partially run down the sides of the pottery, adding a new feature to the decoration.

Hull's Modern ovenproof kitchenware line was introduced with a plaid decorative motif prior to the destruction of the company plant. The intention was to use the Modern line for a wide variety of wares. After the fire, the Modern line was not pursued, although the molds were used to produce wares for the company's Floral, Vegetable, and Cook 'n' Serve lines that followed.

Modern, plaid decoration.
Grease jar (with lid), salt shaker, and bowl. Covered bowl, 6" high; shaker, 3.5" high; bowl, 5.5" diameter. *Courtesy of the Collection of Betty and Joe Yonis.* Grease jar (lidded), $75-85; shaker, $35-40 set; bowl, $15-16

From 1951 to 1954, Hull produced the Just Right Kitchenware line, an inclusive name covering both the Floral and Vegetable embossed kitchenware patterns. The Floral pattern featured raised flowers air-brushed in yellow, with yellow air-brushed lids embellished with brown banding. The Vegetable line was produced in 1951, featuring the vegetable designs one would expect from the name, but only on one side. The Vegetable line was produced in solid high gloss glaze colors including Coral, Green, and Yellow. Each line included fifteen items, including a cookie jar.

Floral.
Covered bowl, 42; salt & pepper shakers. Bowl, 7.5" diameter. *Courtesy of Michael and Sharon Reinheimer.* 42, $25-30; shakers, $20-25

Floral.
Mixing bowls, 40, 9", 40, 7", and 40, 6" diameters. Lipped mixing bowl, 41, 9" diameter. Salad bowl, 49, 10" diameter. *Courtesy of the Collection of Betty and Joe Yonis.* 9", $30-35; 7", $20-25; 6", $16-17; lipped, $45-50; salad, $55-60

In 1952, the Cook 'n' Serve line was produced, created from a combination of Cinderella and Just Right body forms. These wares were decorated in a variety of air-brushed colors including the combinations pink and coral, brown and yellow, solid mottled green, or high gloss white with black handles and lids. Nineteen pieces, including a cookie jar and both large and small skillet trays, were produced in this line and offered only through A.H. Dorman of New York.

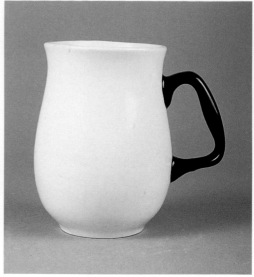

Cook 'n Serve.
White mug with black handle marked Hull, 5.5" high x 3.5" diameter. *Courtesy of the Collection of Betty and Joe Yonis.* $11-12

Cook 'n Serve.
Top: Divided dutch oven with cover, 10" in length.
Bottom: Divided covered casserole, 35.; French handled casserole. 11" and 11.5" in length. *Courtesy of Michael and Sharon Reinheimer.* $25-30 each

Crescent ovenproof kitchenwares had a slightly longer run, produced from 1952 through 1954. Twelve items were offered, including a cookie jar, decorated in either strawberry with maroon trim or chartreuse with dark green trim. An interesting crescent shaped handle gave this line a distinctive look.

Crescent.
Cookie jar with lid, B8, 9.5" high. *Courtesy of the Collection of Betty and Joe Yonis.* $80-90

Crescent.
Teapot, B13, 7.5" high. *Courtesy of the Collection of Betty and Joe Yonis.* $80-90

Hull Pottery Co., Crooksville, Ohio - December 1, 1952

"Crescent Oven-Proof Kitchenware"

Decoration #1 -- Chartreuse - Forest Green Trim
         #2 -- Strawberry - Maroon Trim

	Packed	Weight	Price Doz.
B1-5½" Mixing or Cereal Bowl	4 Doz.	40 lbs.	$ 2.58
B1-7½" Mixing Bowl	2 "	35 "	4.56
B1-9½" Mixing Bowl	1 "	32 "	7.32
B1-3 pc. Mixing Bowl Set	6 Sets	35 "	1.20 Per S
B1-C Casserole and Cover	1 Doz.	32 "	10.50
B2-Casserole and Cover	1 Doz.	40 "	12.72
B4-5 Salt and Pepper Shakers	1 "	8 "	11.40 Doz.
B7-Individual Casserole and Cover	2 "	30 "	6.72
B4-5-7 3pc. Range Set	6 Sets	16 "	1.56 Per S
B8-Cookie Jar and Cover	½ Doz.	25 "	15.72
B13-Teapot and Cover (6 cup)	½ "	18 "	15.48
B13-J Ice Jug (6 cup)	½ "	15 "	12.30
B14-Sugar and Cover	1 "	15 "	7.38
B15-Creamer	1 "	12 "	5.88
B13-14-15 Tea Set	4 Sets	20 "	2.40 Per S
B16-Mug	1 Doz.	12 "	5.76
B5232 - 93 Pc. Assortment - Consisting of:	6 Pkgs.	130 "	52.32 Per A

          3 only (B1 5½-7½-9½") Sets
          ½ Doz. B2 Casserole and Cover
          6 Sets B4-5 Salt and Pepper
          2 Doz. B7 Individual Casserole and Cover
          ½ Doz. B8 Cookie Jar and Cover
          4 only (B13-14-15) Tea Sets
          1 Doz. B16 Mug

Terms 1% 15 days net 30 - F.O.B. Factory, no extra packing charge

Sold only in Standard Packages

The Crescent ovenproof kitchenware line advertisement and listing dated December 1, 1952. Two glaze treatments were listed: #1—Chartreuse with Forest Green Trim; #2—Strawberry with Maroon Trim. A 93 piece assortment was offered. *Courtesy of the Collection of Betty and Joe Yonis.*

Crescent.
Individual covered casserole, B7; sugar bowl, B14; and creamer, B15.
Casserole, 6.25" in length. *Courtesy of Michael and Sharon Reinheimer.*
B7, $15-16; B14, $20-25; B15, $20-25

Debonair kitchenwares had even more "leg" to them, remaining on the market from 1952 to 1955. Debonair was a no-nonsense streamlined line decorated in a high gloss duo-tone lavender and pink with black banding, a solid high gloss chartreuse, or a wine and chartreuse combination.

Debonair.
Coffee/teapot (lid missing), 013; creamer, 014; sugar, 015; individual covered casserole, 07; salt & pepper shakers, 04 & 05 respectively. Teapot, 7" high. *Courtesy of the Collection of Betty and Joe Yonis.* Coffee/teapot, $45-50 (complete); cream & sugar, $11-12 each; individual casserole, $11-12; shakers, $20-25 set.

Debonair.
Coffee/teapot, 013, 7" high; creamer, 014; sugar, 015. *Courtesy of the Collection of Betty and Joe Yonis.* Coffee/teapot, $45-50 (complete); cream & sugar, $11-12 each

In c. 1958, Hull offered both the Heritageware and Marcrest kitchenware lines. Heritageware was decorated in a variety of semi-matte or high gloss glazes, trimmed with the aforementioned "foam edge." Marcrest kitchenwares were produced as promotionals for Marshall Burns and may well have actually been produced outside of the Hull factory walls. These promotional wares were decorated in high gloss pastel glazes and used a number of the Heritageware body shapes to complete the line. (Gick-Burke 1993, 9; Roberts 1980, pp. 19-23; Roberts 1992, pp. 68-78)

Heritageware.
Salt & pepper shakers. *Courtesy of the Collection of Betty and Joe Yonis.* $20-25

Heritageware.
Back: salad bowl, 10"
long.
Front: large pitcher, A-6, 7"
high to lip; small pitcher; a
lidless vinegar or oil cruet;
small bowl. *Courtesy of the
Collection of Betty and Joe
Yonis.* Back: $17-18. Front:
pitcher, A6, $35-40; small
pitcher, $25-30; cruet
(missing lid), $25-30; small
bowl, $10-11

Novelties

Novelty lines and florist wares were also quite popular, whether introduced before the fire or during the 1950s. Novelty pieces came in many forms, with many purposes, ranging from banks to planters. Piggy banks are much in demand. Small dime banks, larger Corky Pig banks (introduced in 1957), and impressively large Jumbo Corky Pig (a.k,a. razorback) piggy banks display an impressive range of design and glaze treatment that keeps collectors hunting for many years. Once introduced, other novelty lines remained in production until the company's end in 1986.

Banks

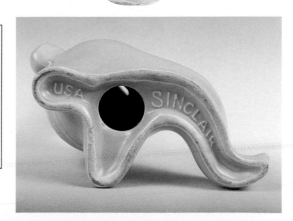

Novelty.
Sinclair Dinosaur bank. This
was a premium made in the
early 1960s for the Sinclair
Oil Company. 7" high.
*Courtesy of the Collection of
Betty and Joe Yonis.* $3500-
3850

Novlety.
Two piggy banks with different cold paint floral motifs, produced in the 1940s. 14" long. *Courtesy of the Collection of Betty and Joe Yonis*. $150-165 each

Novelty.
Pig planter and bank. 8" long. *Courtesy of the Collection of Betty and Joe Yonis*. Planter: $55-60; bank: $200-220

Novelty.
Rare (nickel) piggy bank. 6.5" high. *Courtesy of the Collection of Betty and Joe Yonis.* $500-550

Novelty.
Extremely rare Avocado dime bank. A workman's special. *Courtesy of the Collection of Betty and Joe Yonis.* $450-500.

Novelty.
Three Corky Pig banks and two "dime banks." Dime banks, 5" long. The right dime bank is a commemorative dating from 1996 (date on back of bank). The commemorative is much heavier than the original, which was introduced in 1958. *Courtesy of Michael and Sharon Reinheimer.* Back Corky Pigs, left to right: $115-125; $145-160; $150-165. Front dime banks, left to right: $300-330; (commemorative), $75-85

Left and below:
Novelty.
Three rabbit cotton ball dispensers, 968, 6.25" high. *Courtesy of Michael and Sharon Reinheimer.* $25-30 each

Novelty.
Miniature rabbit salt and pepper shakers, 3" high. *Courtesy of the Collection of Betty and Joe Yonis.* $60-70

Novelty.
Elephant figure and planter. Rare in green. 6" high. *Courtesy of the Collection of Betty and Joe Yonis.* Green, $150-165; yellow, $75-85

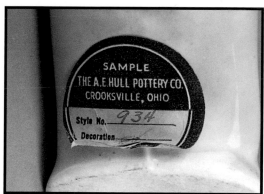

SAMPLE
THE A.E. HULL POTTERY CO.
CROOKSVILLE, OHIO
Style No. 934
Decoration

Left and above:
Novelty.
Elephant planter with an attached A.E. Hull sample sticker, 5.5" high. *Courtesy of Michael and Sharon Reinheimer.* $50-55

Novelty.
Cat doorstop. 7.5" long x 7.25" high. Rare. *Courtesy of the Collection of Betty and Joe Yonis.* $250-275

Novelty.
Poodle planter, 38, copyright 1955, 6.25" high. *Courtesy of Thomas F. and Heather A. Evans.* $75-85

Novelty.
Chinese Chicken planter, 95, 9.5" long. *Courtesy of Michael and Sharon Reinheimer.* $125-135

Novelty.
Duck planters, 104, 11" in length & 79, 7.5"
in length. *Courtesy of Michael and Sharon
Reinheimer.* 104, $65-75; 79, $45-50

Novelty.
Bandana ducks, 74, 75, 76,
9", 6", & 4" long. *Courtesy of
Michael and Sharon
Reinheimer.* 74, $40-45; 75,
$30-35; 76, $20-25

Novelty.
Bandana ducks, 75, 76, & 77
(candleholders). The candleholders are
particularly hard to find and measures 4"
long. *Courtesy of Michael and Sharon
Reinheimer.* 75, $30-35; 76, $20-25; 77,
$60-70

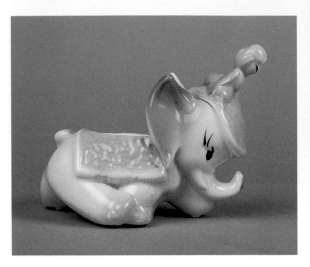

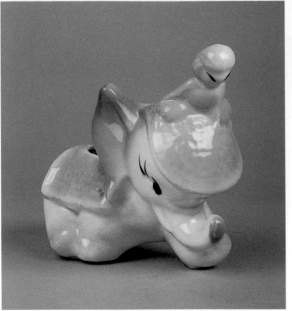

Above and above right:
Novelty.
Elephant planter with rider, 6" long. *Courtesy of Michael and Sharon Reinheimer.* $30-35

Right:
Novelty.
Duck salt and pepper shakers.
5.5" high. *Courtesy of the Collection of Betty and Joe Yonis.* $500-550

Novlety.
Left: Hull elephant planter, 10". There is some question as to whether the small elephant planter on the right was produced by Hull, 6" long. *Courtesy of the Collection of Betty and Joe Yonis.* Large: $200-220

Novelty.
Twin geese planter, 95, 7.5" high. *Courtesy of Michael and Sharon Reinheimer.* $35-40

Novelty.
Long neck geese planters and ashtray/planters, (tall) 411, 12.5" high; (small) 5.5" high. *Courtesy of Michael and Sharon Reinheimer.* Planters, $50-55; ashtrays/planters, $20-25

Novelty.
Handled goose baskets, 413, 10.5" high. *Courtesy of the Collection of Betty and Joe Yonis.* $80-90

Novelty.
Double hippo planter, 81, 8" long; hippo flower frog, 83, 6.25"
long. *Courtesy of Michael and Sharon Reinheimer.* Double hippo,
$125-135; hippo flower frog, $100-110

Novelty.
Parrots pulling cart planters, 313 (large), 60 (small), 12.5" & 9.5"
long. *Courtesy of Michael and Sharon Reinheimer.* 313, $100-110;
60, $25-30

Novelty.
Pig planter, 39, 6.25" high. *Courtesy of the Collection of Betty and Joe Yonis.* $70-80

Novelty.
Rooster lamp, 6" high. *Courtesy of the Collection of Betty and Joe Yonis.* $150-165

Novelty.
Rooster planter, 53, 6" high. *Courtesy of the Collection of Betty and Joe Yonis.* $30-35

Novelty.
Hull Rooster planters, 951, 7" high. *Courtesy of the Collection of Betty and Joe Yonis.* $125-135 each

People

Novelty.
Toothpick holder, figural, 3.75" high.
This is a sample piece. *Courtesy of the Collection of Betty and Joe Yonis.*
$500-550

Novelty.
Strike up the band! Early Swing Band 6" high novelty figures. There are two additional figures, a drummer straddling a large bass drum and a band leader (who has no instrument and has one hand up away from his chest to keep time). The drummer figure was used to create a unique figure (a man riding a grinning donkey) for Franklin D. Roosevelt. *Courtesy of the Collection of Betty and Joe Yonis.* Left to right: $160-175 each.

Novelty.
This figure is a combination of an altered "Swing Band" drummer and novelty donkey planter. Produced for Franklin D. Roosevelt. 7.5" high x 7" long. *Courtesy of the Collection of Betty and Joe Yonis.* $2200-2420

Novelty.
Boy and boy on fence planters. Boy: 5.75" high; boy on fence: 7" long. *Courtesy of Michael and Sharon Reinheimer.* $20-25 & $25-30 respectively

Novelty.
Child's head planter, 62, 6" high. It is very unusual to find this piece with the cold paint intact. *Courtesy of the Collection of Betty and Joe Yonis.* $175-190

Novelty.
Basket Girl planters, 954, marked Hull Art. *Courtesy of Michael and Sharon Reinheimer.* $25-30

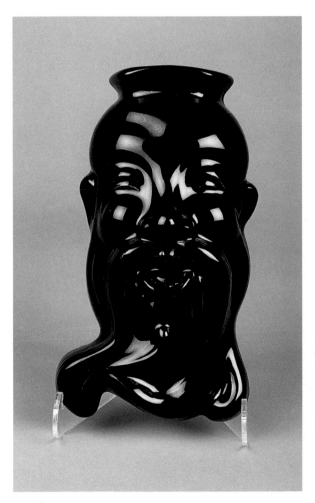

Novelty.
Chinese Sage Mask wall pocket, 120, 8" high. *Courtesy of Michael and Sharon Reinheimer.* $75-85

Novlety.
Rare matte colors on this 8" high novelty Basket Girl, 954. *Courtesy of the Collection of Betty and Joe Yonis.* $125-135

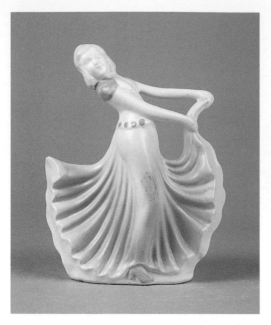

Novelty.
Dancing Girl, 955, 7.25" high. *Courtesy of the Collection of Betty and Joe Yonis.* $55-60

Novelty.
Clown planters, 82, 6.25". *Courtesy of Michael and Sharon Reinheimer.* Left to right: $50-55; $35-40

Novelty.
Knight planters, 55, 7" high each. *Courtesy of Michael and Sharon Reinheimer.* $65-75 each

Imperial

Finally, in 1955 a line was introduced that would remain influential throughout the rest of the company's production history. The Imperial line was a very broad line of florist wares. If you could put potting soil in it, Hull made it! Both satin and high gloss glazes were used to decorate these wares. Novel designs were frequently found among Imperial's planters and pots as well.

Chain Store Lines

Chain stores frequently purchased wares in a variety of mold shapes in a variety of glaze treatments but without any decoration beyond the glazing. These wares (vast collections of artwares, novelty items, and florist wares) were frequently produced and sold to the chain stores without carrying any Hull manufacturer's marks.

Chain Store Lines of the 1950s: A Sampler

These lines included an assortment of wares, often pulled from a number of established lines.

Regal	1952-1960
Royal: a.k.a. Mist	1955-1957
Sun Valley Pastels	1956-1957
Fantasy	1957-1958
Fiesta	1957-1958
Flowerware	1957-1958
Jubilee	1957
Mayfair	1958-1959
Coronet	1959
Gold-Medal Flowerware	1959

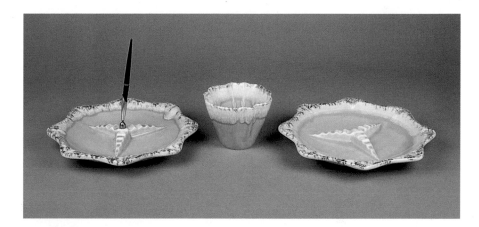

Coronet, 1959.
Ashtrays (one mounted with a pen), A5, 11" in length; flower pot, 204, 4" high. *Courtesy of Thomas F. and Heather A. Evans.* A5, $45-50; A5 with pen, $55-60; 204, $20-25

Fiesta, 1957-1958.
Pedestal planter, 43, 6.25" high. Marked Hull USA 43. *Courtesy of the Collection of Betty and Joe Yonis.* $40-45

Fantasy/Fiesta, 1957-1958.
Ashtray/planter combination in a black metal stand sold to chain stores through the Fantasy or Fiesta lines. 26" high. *Courtesy of Michael and Sharon Reinheimer.* $50-55

Later Years and Wares, 1960s-1986

From the 1960s onward, Hull turned away from the artwares, concentrating largely on two very broad lines: the Imperial florist wares introduced in 1955 and the House 'n Garden Serving-wares begun in 1960. In 1978, with the death of James Brannon Hull, Henry Sulens took up the company presidency while Robert W. Hull acted as Chairman of the Board of Directors. In 1981, Larry Taylor would replace Henry Sulens as president. Taylor would oversee the introduction of several new dinner-ware lines in new forms during the company's final years. These were offered in an attempt to bolster lagging sales as the company struggled under the dual burdens of increased foreign competition and internal union unrest. Including among these last lines were the Ridge Collection (Flint Ridge, Tawny Ridge, and Walnut Ridge), Heartland, and Country Belle. Despite these final offerings, the Hull Pottery Company of Crooksville, Ohio, ceased its operations in March 1986.

Imperial and Other Florist Wares

Introduced in 1955, prodigious quantities of baskets, flower bowls, garden dishes, novelty planters, urn vases (jardinieres), and vases would continue to be produced for the Imperial florist ware line throughout the remainder of the company's history. Wares in the Imperial line were produced both with and without the foam edge. An interesting variation of nine Imperial shapes was experimented with briefly but never offered to the public. This was the Supreme line, decorated with scored and scraped surface decoration described as "tooled." Supreme was glazed in either Agate and Chartreuse or Ripe Olive and Orange.

Left and above:
An advertisement for the Imperial "Supreme" line: "Sculptured Designs by Louise." The line is shown in both the Agate & Chartreuse and Ripe Olive & Orange glazes. Items in the line include: No. 1 Bud Vase, 8"; No. 2 Urn, 5.5" diameter x 5.75" high; No. 3 Jardiniere, 5.75" diameter x 4.5" high; No. 4. Footed Bowl, 7.5" diameter x 4.5" high; No. 5 Basket, 8.75"; No. 6 Candy Box, 6.25" diameter x 7" high; No. 7 Pedestal Vase, 10"; No. 8 Jug, 5.5" diameter x 9.5" high; No. 9 Exotic Vase, 12.25". *Courtesy of the Collection of Betty and Joe Yonis.*

Imperial—"Designed Especially for Florists."
Four Imperial planters decorated with Mirror Brown glaze and a foam edge. Left basket, F67, 8.5" high; unmarked strawberry basket planter, 7" high; lower planter bowl with Indian designs, F 65, 3.75" high x 6" diameter; vase, F58, 5.5" high. *Courtesy of Michael and Sharon Reinheimer.* F67, $100-110; strawberry basket, $125-135; F65, $75-85; F58, $50-55

Imperial.
Supreme. Jug, 8, 9.5" high. *Courtesy of the Collection of Betty and Joe Yonis.* $175-190

Imperial.
Supreme. Jug, 8, 9.5" high. *Courtesy of the Collection of Betty and Joe Yonis.* $175-190

*F66

* F66 Oval Handled Basket
7'' × 7'' High

* F67 Wicker Embossed Handled Basket
7½'' Long × 8'' High

Baskets are always best sellers! Richly embossed floral and wicker patterns make them outstanding complements to every arrangement. Like the entire Imperial line, they are available in deep green, warm brown or satiny white to give them instant and long-lasting appeal.

† B36 Footed Basket
7'' Diameter × 9'' High

(Flowers and Macrame not included)

Above and right:
Imperial Florist Ware catalog by the Hull Pottery Company.
Courtesy of the Collection of Betty and Joe Yonis.

† Best-Selling Carry-Over Items
* New Items

† F469 Paneled Garden Dish
7¾'' × 4¾'' × 3¼''

† F75 Garden Dish
6½'' × 3⅜'' × 2¾''

† F467 Fluted Garden Dish
7'' × 4½'' × 3''

† F76 Garden Dish
7'' × 4'' × 3½''

† F17 Daisy Embossed Garden Dish
7¾'' × 4¾'' × 3¼''

† F18 Fruit Embossed Garden Dish
8¾'' × 4¾'' × 3¼''

Be imaginative!

Create your own atmosphere with our planters. Choose the style and color you want. Hard-to-arrange florals will always look their best in Imperial pottery.

† F5 Swirl Goblet Planter
4¾'' High

† F88 Sculptured Pedestal Planter
5¼'' × 5⅝''

* F56 Footed Six-Sided Planter
5'' × 5'' High

* F55 Footed Six-Sided Planter
5¼'' × 3¼''

* F62 Eight-Sided Footed Bowl
7'' × 3¾'' High

A54 Round Pedestal Planter
4'' Diameter Top × 5'' High

† Best-Selling Carry-Over Items
* New Items
(Floral arrangements not included)

Floral gifts in planters are gifts not soon forgotten. Long after the first arrangement has lost its color, a planter continues to be useful and appreciated. Planters are never out of fashion and are at home in just about every decor.

*F54   *F50   *F34
*F53   *F49   *F63

* F54 Footed Round Bowl With Lugs
5'' Diameter × 3½'' High

* F53 Footed Round Bowl
5½'' Diameter × 3½'' High

* F50 Round Pedestal Planter
5'' Diameter × 3½'' High

* F49 Round Pedestal Planter
3¾'' Diameter × 3'' High

† F34 Urn Shaped Planter
4¾'' Diameter × 5'' High

* F63 Oval Footed Bowl
7½'' × 4¾'' × 4'' High

† I-21 Oval Fluted Garden Dish
8'' × 5½'' × 3''

* F60 Round Paneled Bowl
7'' Diameter × 3¾'' High

† B6 Fancy Ruffled Bowl
7¾'' × 3¾'' High

* F59 Round Paneled Bowl
6'' Diameter × 3¾'' High

Many items in the Imperial line are ideal for hanging baskets but take special note that we do **not** furnish the macrame commonly used for hanging basket purposes. The two items F65 and F66 illustrated as hanging baskets show only their adaptable usage, the same as illustrated flowers and vegetables.

† F10 Fluted Round Flower Bowl
6½'' Diameter × 3¾'' High

* F65 Embossed Round Bowl
6'' Diameter × 3½'' High

† A2 Square Footed Planter
5" Square × 3½" High

* F58 Vase With Flared Top
5¼" High

Designed for you.

Whether formal or casual, our varied selection of shapes and colors lets you meet all your customers' needs. That will mean greater satisfaction for them and increased sales for you.

* F64 Oval Vase
6½" High

† Best-Selling Carry-Over Items
* New Items

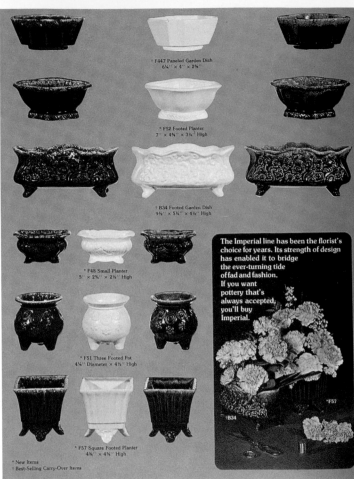

† F447 Paneled Garden Dish
6¼" × 4" × 2¾"

* F52 Footed Planter
7" × 4¾" × 3¼" High

† B34 Footed Garden Dish
9½" × 5¼" × 4½" High

* F48 Small Planter
5" × 2¾" × 2½" High

* F51 Three Footed Pot
4¼" Diameter × 4½" High

* F57 Square Footed Planter
4¾" × 4¾" High

The Imperial line has been the florist's choice for years. Its strength of design has enabled it to bridge the ever-turning tide of fad and fashion. If you want pottery that's always accepted, you'll buy Imperial.

* F57

† B34

* New Items
† Best-Selling Carry-Over Items

† F404 Footed Garden Dish
7" × 4" × 3"

† F405 Footed Flower Dish
8¼" × 4½" × 3¼"

† F78 Rectangular Leaf Design Garden Dish
10½" × 5¼" × 3¾"

† F47 Rectangular Garden Dish
11¾" × 4¾" × 4"

* F70 Caricature Frog
7" Wide × 6¼" High

Hull's Aquatic Animals

Our aquatic animals will be pets in any setting. Their cheerful presence is perfect for rec-rooms, centerpieces or informal arrangements.

* F58 Caricature Hippo Planter
8½" Long × 5" Wide × 4½" High

* F71 Swan
9" Long × 5½" Wide × 8" High

* F69 Duck Planter
10" Long × 5½" Wide × 5¼" High

The Imperial Line offers a large variety of shapes and the three most popular underglaze color combinations which may be mixed in cartons at no extra cost. But the total quantities per carton as indicated in our price list remain standard.

Imperial
by Hull

† F42 Rectangular Fluted Garden Dish
8½" × 5" × 3¼"

† F83 Pressed Pedestal Planter
6" Diameter × 3½" High

† F39 Fluted Oval Garden Dish
7" × 4¼" × 2¼"

† Best-Selling Carry-Over Items
(Florals not included)

Above and left:
Imperial Florist Ware catalog by the Hull Pottery Company.
Courtesy of the Collection of Betty and Joe Yonis.

Imperial.
Small Tangerine glazed planter, F48, 2.5" high x
5" long. *Courtesy of Michael and Sharon
Reinheimer.* $20-25

Imperial/Miscellaneous.
Ashtray/planter combination in a black metal stand. 26" high.
Courtesy of Michael and Sharon Reinheimer. $50-55

Imperial/Miscellaneous.
Imperial flower pots in a brass stand measuring
33" high. *Courtesy of Michael and Sharon
Reinheimer.* $100-110

Imperial/Novelty.
Boy planter, F94, 8" high; dolphin novelty planter (not Imperial, possibly Medley), 810;
chickadee planter, F474, 5.25" high. *Courtesy of Michael and Sharon Reinheimer.* F94,
$40-45; 810, $40-45; F474, $20-25

Imperial.
Caricature Frog planters, F70, 6.5" high. *Courtesy of Michael and Sharon Reinheimer.*
Left to right: $100-125; $50-60; $35-40

Imperial.
Three hippo planters, F68, 9" long. *Courtesy of Michael and Sharon Reinheimer.*
Brown, $125-135; White, $35-40; Agate, $50-55

Imperial.
Swan planters/centerpieces, F812, 8" high x 9" long. *Courtesy of Michael and Sharon Reinheimer.* Left to right: $50-55; $40-45; $25-30; $100-110; $50-55

Imperial.
Swan ashtrays/planters, F815, 4.5" high x 4" long. *Courtesy of the Collection of Betty and Joe Yonis.* $40-45 each

Imperial.
Seven baby swan planters/ashtrays, the top two left hand examples are in common colors. The rest are rare. F21, 4.5" long each. *Courtesy of the Collection of Betty and Joe Yonis.* Most common: $25-30; rarest: $100-110

Imperial.
Llama "Unusual Planter,"
F80, 11.5" long x 9.25"
high. *Courtesy of Lyle
Applegate.* $100-110

Imperial/Miscellaneous.
Madonnas, right: F7. 5"
and 7.25" high respectively.
*Courtesy of Michael and
Sharon Reinheimer.* $10
11; $20-25

Chain Store Lines

Through the 1960s, Hull Pottery continued to offer vase, planter, and novelty assortments to the chain stores under a variety of names. Among these were Athena, Coronet, Medley, and Flower Club. These were offered in a variety of glazes, both with and without a foam edge. Pieces of special interest include the Athena wall pocket/picture frame planter, the Medley dolphin, swan, and teddy bear planters and cat vase, and Flower Club's three swans and Madonna pieces.

Athena.
Picture frame wall pocket, 611, 8.5" high. *Courtesy of Michael and Sharon Reinheimer.* $75-85

Flower Club Ceramics/Imperial.
Flower Club Ceramics flower basket, 822; Imperial flower basket, F 38. *Courtesy of Michael and Sharon Reinheimer.* 822, $25-30; F38, $20-25

Serving-wares
House 'n Garden

The House 'n Garden line was heavy, streamlined, simple table and kitchenware conveniently described as Serving-ware. The form and ware types in this line were the result of a movement throughout the twentieth century toward simplification in dinner wares. In the early decades of the century, the superabundance of serving and dining pieces (including bone dishes, butter pats, and any number of complex Victorian wares) was stripped away and the forms were simplified and streamlined, following Art Deco styling in the 1920s and 1930s. These early wares ushered in the American age of "casual dining." Vibrant solid colored glazes were employed among these early wares, and consumers were encouraged to mix and match the different colors among their table settings. Hull's House 'n Garden line would follow this tried-and-true format decades later in 1961 when introducing their Rainbow Serving-ware glaze colors, including Butterscotch, Green Agate, and Tangerine.

House 'n Garden Ovenproof Serving-ware Rainbow.
Rainbow tray and soup mug sets glazed in Tangerine, Butterscotch, Green Agate and Mirror Brown–all with a foam edge, 553 & 554. *Courtesy of Michael and Sharon Reinheimer.* $35-40 sets

In the 1940s and 1950s, tablewares had been further smoothed and stylized by Russel Wright and his *American Modern* dinnerware. Wright's flattened, gently curving forms and curled rims utilized the plasticity of clay to create innovative forms. The simple, heavy forms of the House 'n Garden line followed in these traditions. This ware was also quite sturdy and designed for everyday use, another requirement of wares destined for "casual dining."

When the House 'n Garden Serving-ware line was first introduced in 1960 it was glazed in Mirror Brown trimmed with an ivory/white foam edge. The Rainbow colors were added a year later, among others, providing a welcomed diversity to the line. The popularity of this line is evident in the fact that over one hundred pieces, including cookie jars, were produced in the line's twenty-five year run.

A detailed advertising packet for the House 'n Garden Serving-ware line in Mirror Brown glaze trimmed in Ivory Foam. This packet of material was dated from 1969. Note the covered carafe, 505, which fits snugly into the 7 oz. coffee cup, with its deep well saucer, to become the four piece coffee carafe set, 528. *Courtesy of the Collection of Betty and Joe Yonis.*

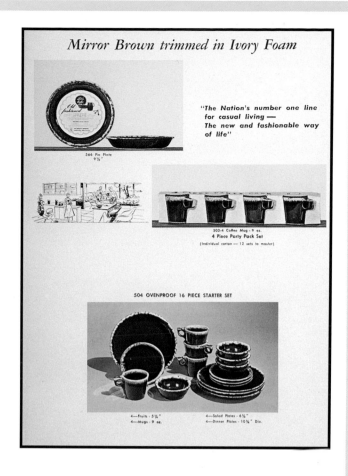

A detailed advertising packet for the House 'n Garden Serving-ware line in Mirror Brown glaze trimmed in Ivory Foam. This packet of material was dated from 1969. Note the covered carafe, 505, which fits snugly into the 7 oz. coffee cup, with its deep well saucer, to become the four piece coffee carafe set, 528. *Courtesy of the Collection of Betty and Joe Yonis.*

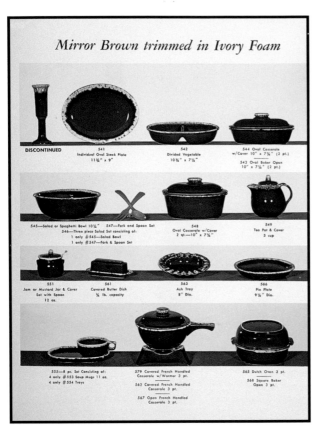

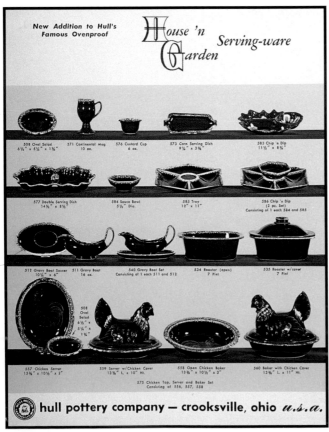

A detailed advertising packet for the House 'n Garden Serving-ware line in Mirror Brown glaze trimmed in Ivory Foam. This packet of material was dated from 1969. Note the covered carafe, 505, which fits snugly into the 7 oz. coffee cup, with its deep well saucer, to become the four piece coffee carafe set, 528. *Courtesy of the Collection of Betty and Joe Yonis.*

Hull Pottery Co., Crooksville, Ohio 43731

HOUSE 'N GARDEN SERVING-WARE
Mirror Brown trimmed in Ivory Foam

July 14, 1969

OVENPROOF

#6036—86 Piece Introductory Assortment Featuring New Items

QUANTITY ASSORTMENT	DESCRIPTION	APPROX. WEIGHT	PRICE DOZEN	PRICE ASST.
1/3 doz.	535 Roaster w/Cover 7 pt.	25 lbs.	$24.00	$ 8.00
4 only	540 Gravy Boat Set	12 lbs.	1.60 set	6.40
	consisting of: 1 each: 511-512			
2 only	559 Server w/Chicken Cover 13-3/8" L. x 10" Hi.	22 lbs.	3.65 each	7.30
2 only	560 Baker w/Chicken Cover 13-3/8" L. x 11" Hi.	23 lbs.	3.75 each	7.50
1 doz.	571 Continental Mug 10 oz.	15 lbs	6.60	6.60
1 doz.	573 Corn Serving Dish 9-1/4" x 3-3/8"	11 lbs.	4.20	4.20
2 doz.	576 Custard Cup 6 oz.	10 lbs.	2.28	4.56
1/3 doz.	577 Double Serving Dish 14-1/2" x 8-1/2"	15 lbs.	19.20	6.40
1/6 doz.	583 Chip 'n Dip 11-1/2" x 8-3/4"	5 lbs.	13.20	2.20
4 only	586 Chip 'n Dip (2 pc. set) consisting of: 1 each: 584-585	15 lbs.	1.80 set	7.20

86 Pieces (Including covers) $60.36

Approximate weight—153 lbs.

Terms: 1% 15 days net 30—fob Crooksville, Ohio

Hull Pottery Co., Crooksville, Ohio 43731

Page 2.

Mirror Brown House 'n Garden—continued

ITEM NO.	DESCRIPTION	PACKED	APPROX. WEIGHT	PRICE DOZEN
530	Saucer 5-1/2"	2 doz.	17 lb.	$ 2.52
531	Plate 8-1/2"	1 doz.	17 lb.	5.52
532	12 Pc. Luncheon Set—consisting of:	1 set	13 lb.	3.62 set
	4 only 529 Cups 6 oz.			
	4 only 530 Saucers 5-1/2"			
	4 only 531 Luncheon Plates 8-1/2"			
533	Fruit 6"	2 doz.	21 lb.	3.12
536	Mixing Bowl 6"	3 doz.	41 lb.	3.60
537	Mixing Bowl 7"	2 doz.	41 lb.	4.68
538	Mixing Bowl w/Pouring Spout 8"	1 doz.	29 lb.	5.64
539	3 Pc. Mixing Bowl Set (6", 7", 8")	6 sets	31 lb.	1.26 set
541	Individual Oval Steak Plate 11-3/4" x 9"	1 doz.	27 lb.	7.56
542	Divided Vegetable Dish 10-3/4" x 7-1/4"	1/2 doz.	15 lb.	10.08
543	Oval Baker 10" x 7-1/4"	1/2 doz.	13 lb.	8.04
544	Oval Casserole w/cover 2 pt.	1/2 doz.	21 lb.	11.76
545	Salad or Spaghetti Bowl 10-1/4"	1/3 doz.	13 lb.	12.00
546	3 Pc. Salad Set—Consisting of:	4 sets	13 lb.	1.26 set
	1 only 545 Salad Bowl 10-1/4"			
	1 only 547—Fork & Spoon Set			
547	Fork and Spoon Set	12 sets	2 lb.	.42 set
548	Deep Oval Casserole and cover 2 qt.	1/3 doz.	17 lb.	15.96
549	Tea Pot and cover 5 cup	1/2 doz.	14 lb.	10.08
550	Jam or Mustard Jar and cover 12 oz.	2 doz.	21 lb.	4.56
551	Jam or Mustard Jar and Cover Set consisting of:	24 sets	21 lb.	.48 set
	1 only 550—Jam or Mustard Jar and Cover			
	1 only 552—Crystal Plastic Spoon			
552	Jam or Mustard Spoon/Crystal Plastic	2 doz.	1/2 lb.	1.47
553	Soup Mug 11 oz.	2 doz.	23 lb.	4.08
554	Tray 9-1/2" x 5-3/4"	2 doz.	27 lb.	5.64
555	8 Pc. Soup 'n Sandwich Set consisting of:	1 set	8 lb.	3.34 set
	4 only 553 Soup Mugs 11 oz.			
	4 only 554 Trays			
561	Covered Butter Dish (1/4 lb. capacity)	1 doz.	18 lb.	7.32
562	3 Pt. Covered French Hdld. Casserole	1/3 doz.	18 lb.	13.80
563	Ash Tray 8" dia.	1 doz.	18 lb.	6.36
564	Candle Flame Warmer & Candle	1/2 doz.	11 lb.	8.40
565	Dutch Oven 8-3/4" x 9-1/2" x 2-1/2"—consists of: (2 only 568 Square Bakers)	1/2 doz.	30 lb.	17.04
566	Pie Plate 9-1/4" dia.	1 doz.	24 lb.	6.96
567	Open French Hdld. Casserole 3 pt.	1/3 doz.	12 lb.	10.08
568	Square Baker 3 pt.	1 doz.	30 lb.	8.52
569	6-1/2" Soup or Salad Bowl	2 doz.	29 lb.	4.56
570	Starter Set consisting of:	1 set	15 lb.	4.73 set
	4 only 533 Fruits 6"			
	4 only 597 Cups 7 oz.			
	4 only 598 Saucers 5-7/8"			
	4 only 599 Plates 9-3/8"			
572	Jumbo Stein 32 oz.	1 doz.	25 lb.	7.32

"Terms of Sale" appear at bottom of page 3

Hull Pottery Co., Crooksville, Ohio 43731

November 1, 1969

HOUSE 'N GARDEN SERVING-WARE
Mirror Brown, trimmed in Ivory Foam

OVENPROOF

"the nation's number one line for casual living"—the new and fashionable way of life"

ITEM NO.	DESCRIPTION	PACKED	APPROX. WEIGHT	PRICE DOZEN
500	Dinner Plate 10-1/4" Dia.	1 doz.	24 lb.	$ 6.96
501	Salad Plate 6-1/2" Dia.	2 doz.	18 lb.	2.52
502	Mug 9 oz.	4 doz.	40 lb.	3.36
502-4	Coffee Mug 9 oz. 4 Piece Party Pack Set (Individual carton—12 sets to master)	12 sets	40 lb.	1.22 set
503	Fruit 5-1/4"	2 doz.	21 lb.	2.52
504	Starter Set consisting of:	1 set	17 lb.	4.83 set
	4 only 500 Dinner Plate 10-1/4"			
	4 only 501 Salad Plate 6-1/2"			
	4 only 502 Mug 9 oz.			
	4 only 503 Fruit 5-1/4"			
505	Carafe w/cover 2 cup	1 doz.	14 lb.	6.96
506	Open Baker 32 oz.	1 doz.	21 lb.	6.84
507	Casserole w/cover 32 oz.	1 doz.	30 lb.	8.64
509	Water Jug 5 pt. (old fashioned)	1/2 doz.	22 lb.	12.60
510	Bean Pot w/cover 2 qt.	1/2 doz.	21 lb.	12.60
513	French Handled Casserole 12 oz.	2 doz.	21 lb.	3.36
514	Ice Jug 2 qt.	1/2 doz.	17 lb.	11.40
515	Salt Shaker w/cork 3-3/4" Hi.	2 doz.	15 lb.	3.72
516	Pepper Shaker w/cork 3-3/4" Hi.	2 doz.	15 lb.	3.72
517	Salt & Pepper Set	12 sets	15 lb.	.63 set
518	Creamer	2 doz.	18 lb.	3.24
519	Sugar Bowl w/cover 12 oz.	2 doz.	21 lb.	4.56
520	Sugar & Creamer Set	12 sets	20 lb.	.65 set
521	Leaf Shaped Chip 'n Dip	1/3 doz.	13 lb.	20.16
522	Coffee Pot w/cover 8 cup	1/2 doz.	20 lb.	20.16
523	Cookie Jar w/cover 94 oz.	1/2 doz.	23 lb.	15.96
524	Individual Bean Pot w/cover 12 oz.	2 doz.	21 lb.	4.56
525	Jug 2 pt.	1 doz.	21 lb.	6.96
526	Beer Stein 16 oz.	2 doz.	28 lb.	4.80
526-4	Beer Stein 16 oz. 4 Piece Party Pack Set (Individual carton—6 sets to master)	6 sets	30 lb.	1.79 set
527	Covered French Hdld. Casserole 12 oz. (same as 513 except with cover)	2 doz.	33 lb.	4.32
528	4 Pc. Coffee Carafe Set—consisting of:	1 set	3 lb.	1.22 set
	1 only 505 Coffee Carafe w/cover			
	1 only 597 Coffee Cup 7 oz.			
	1 only 598 Saucer 5-7/8"			
529	Cup 6 oz.	4 doz.	32 lb.	3.24

"Terms of Sale" appear at bottom of page 3

Hull Pottery Co., Crooksville, Ohio 43731

Page 3.

Mirror Brown House 'n Garden—continued

ITEM NO.	DESCRIPTION	PACKED	APPROX. WEIGHT	PRICE DOZEN
574	Oval Serving Dish 10" x 5" x 1-5/8" Hi.	2 doz.	28 lb.	$ 6.96
578	12 Pc. Serving-ware Set consisting of:	1 set	17 lb.	4.73 set
	4 only 500 Dinner Plates 10-1/2" dia.			
	4 only 502—9 oz. Mugs			
	4 only 569 Soup or Salad 6-1/2" dia.			
579	French Hdld. Casserole w/cover & warmer	1 set	6-1/2 lb.	2.52 set
580	12 Pc. Serving-ware Set consisting of:	1 set	15 lb.	4.20 set
	4 only 500 Dinner Plates 10-1/4" dia.			
	4 only 502—9 oz. Mugs			
	4 only 503 Fruits 5-1/2" dia.			
590	Individual Leaf Dish 7-1/4" x 4-3/4"	2 doz.	18 lb.	4.68
591	Leaf Shaped Chip 'n Dip 12-1/4" x 9"	1/2 doz.	15 lb.	13.80
592	Hen on Nest Casserole	1/2 doz.	25 lb.	20.16
593	Oval Well 'n Tree Steak Plate 14" x 10"	1/2 doz.	18 lb.	15.12
594	Table size Salt Shaker	2 doz.	9 lb.	3.24
595	Table size Pepper Shaker	2 doz.	9 lb.	3.24
596	Table size Salt & Pepper Set	12 sets	9 lb.	.55 set
597	Cup 7 oz.	4 doz.	27 lb.	3.24
598	Saucer 5-7/8"	2 doz.	14 lb.	2.52
599	Luncheon Plate 9-3/8"	1 doz.	19 lb.	6.12
1095	45 Piece Dinner Set consisting of:	1 set	43 lb.	13.76 set
	8 only 500 Dinner Plate 10-1/4"			
	8 only 501 Salad Plate 6-1/2"			
	8 only 503 Fruit 5-1/4"			
	8 only 529 Cup 6 oz.			
	8 only 530 Saucer 5-1/2"			
	1 only 520 Sugar & Creamer Set			
	1 only 541 Steak Plate 11-3/4" x 9"			
	1 only 542 Divided Vegetable Dish 10-3/4" x 7-1/4"			

HAND DECORATED PIGGY BANKS

195	Corky Piggy Bank	2 doz.	42 lb.	9.00
	Color: Mirror Brown trimmed in Pink / Mirror Brown trimmed in Blue			
196	Sitting Piggy Bank	2 doz.	42 lb.	9.00
	Color: Mirror Brown trimmed in Yellow and Turquoise			

NOTE: #195 and # 196 Corky Piggy Banks may be assorted in a 2 dozen carton

197	Jumbo Corky Piggy Bank	1/2 doz.	20 lb.	21.00
	Color: Mirror Brown trimmed in Yellow and Turquoise			

TERMS OF SALE

Sold only in standard packages—no extra packing charge

Terms: 1% 15 days net 30—fob Crooksville, Ohio

NO ALLOWANCE FOR BREAKAGE—CLAIMS MUST BE FILED WITH COMMON CARRIER

see 600 SERIES LIST FOR ITEMS AVAILABLE IN "AVOCADO"

Items listed in both Mirror Brown and Avocado may be assorted in cartons at no extra cost

An advertisement for the ovenproof House 'n Garden Mirror Brown glazed 16 piece set. *Courtesy of the Collection of Betty and Joe Yonis.*

House 'n Garden Ovenproof Serving-ware.
Rare plate (with stars motif similar to the Bicentennial line) glazed in Mirror Brown trimmed in Ivory Foam. 10.5" diameter. *Courtesy of Lyle Applegate.* $125-135

House 'n Garden Ovenproof Serving-ware.
Rare Hull Mirror Brown divided grill plate, with the letter H dividing the plate, 9.5" diameter *Courtesy of Michael and Sharon Reinheimer.* $150-165

House 'n Garden Ovenproof Serving-ware.
Pie (566) and quiche plates glazed in Mirror Brown trimmed in Ivory Foam. 9.25" and 10" diameters. *Courtesy of Michael and Sharon Reinheimer.* $100-110 each

House 'n Garden Ovenproof
Serving-ware.
Spaghetti dish, oval, 10.5" in length.
Marked Spaghetti on the back. *Courtesy
of Michael and Sharon Reinheimer.*
$35-40

House 'n Garden Ovenproof Serving-ware.
Egg dish, serve all leaf, and spoon rest glazed in Mirror Brown trimmed in Ivory Foam.
9 x 9.5" egg, 12" long serve all, 6.75" spoon rest. *Courtesy of Michael and Sharon
Reinheimer.* Egg dish, $50-55; serve all, $100-110; spoon rest, $40-45

House 'n Garden Ovenproof Serving-ware.
Rectangular salad bowl (hard to find), 583, and alternate style salt and pepper shakers, 596. Salad, 11" across. *Courtesy of Michael and Sharon Reinheimer.* 583, $50-55; 596, $15-16

House 'n Garden Ovenproof Serving-ware.
Chip 'n Dip, 583, 11.5" x 8.75". *Courtesy of Michael and Sharon Reinheimer.* $65-75

House 'n Garden Ovenproof Serving-ware.
Chip 'n Dip two piece set glazed in Mirror Brown with an Ivory Foam Edge, 586, 12" x 11" tray, 5.5" diameter sauce bowl. *Courtesy of Michael and Sharon Reinheimer.* $250-300

House 'n Garden Ovenproof Serving-ware.
Double serving dish, 577, glazed in Mirror Brown trimmed in Ivory Foam. 15" long; heart ashtray, 18, 7" long. *Courtesy of Michael and Sharon Reinheimer.* Double dish, $250-275; ashtray, $100-110

House 'n Garden Ovenproof Serving-ware.
Coffee carafe four piece set, 528, 8" high together. The carafe holds two cups of coffee. *Courtesy of Michael and Sharon Reinheimer.* $50-55

House 'n Garden Ovenproof Serving-ware.
Left to right: water jug (509), jug (two pint, 525), jug or creamer (519), 9", 7", 4.5" high. *Courtesy of Michael and Sharon Reinheimer.* 509, $20-25; 525, $10-11; 519, $5-6

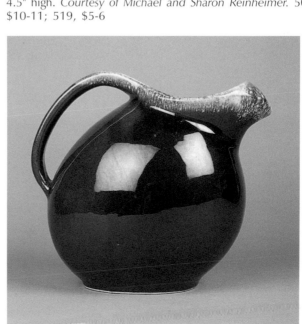

House 'n Garden Ovenproof Serving-ware.
Ice jug (two quart), 514, 7.5" high. *Courtesy of Michael and Sharon Reinheimer.* $20-25

House 'n Garden Ovenproof Serving-ware.
Soufflé dish; corn serving dish, 573; French handled casserole open, 513; oval serving dish, 8.75" in length (this smaller size are harder to find; the larger example measures 10" in length). Soufflé, 9" in length; open casserole, 8" in length; corn dish, 9.5" long. *Courtesy of Michael and Sharon Reinheimer.* Soufflé dish, $100-110; 573, $100-120; 513 (small size), $15-16; oval dish (small size), $15-16

House 'n Garden Ovenproof Serving-ware.
French handled casserole with cover and basket glazed in Mirror Brown trimmed in Ivory Foam, 7.5" long with handle. *Courtesy of Thomas F. and Heather A. Evans.* $15-16

House 'n Garden Ovenproof Serving-ware.
Covered French handled pan casserole with warmer, three pint, 579. Without the warmer, the covered French handled casserole had item number 562 and without the lid, the open French handled casserole had item number 567. *Courtesy of Michael and Sharon Reinheimer.* 579, $75-85

House 'n Garden Ovenproof Serving-ware.
Two quart baker, 567, glazed in Mirror Brown trimmed in Ivory Foam 14" across tab handles. *Courtesy of Thomas F. and Heather A. Evans.* $100-110

House 'n Garden Ovenproof Serving-ware. Two tier tidbit tray and an Imperial heart-shaped garden dish, F61, both glazed in Mirror Brown trimmed in Ivory Foam. 10.5 & 6.75" diameter tidbit trays. 7" garden dish. *Courtesy of Michael and Sharon Reinheimer.* Tidbit tray, $60-70; garden dish, $100-110

House 'n Garden Ovenproof Serving-ware. Baker with chicken cover, 560, chicken server, 557, and oval salad, 508, glazed in Mirror Brown trimmed in Ivory Foam. Covered baker, 11" high; chicken server, 13.25" long; oval salad, 6.5" wide. *Courtesy of Michael and Sharon Reinheimer.* #560, $225-250; #557, $120-130; #508, $50-55

Far left and left:
House 'n Garden Oven-proof Serving-ware.
Hen on Nest casserole marked "Bake and Serve in This Dish," 592, 8" long. *Courtesy of Michael and Sharon Reinheimer.* $50-55

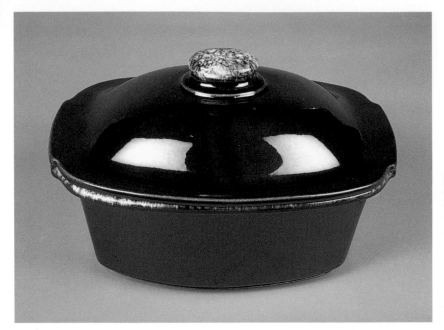

House 'n Garden Ovenproof Serving-ware.
Roaster with cover, 535, 7 pint, glazed in Mirror Brown trimmed in Ivory Foam. 12" long x 7.5" high. *Courtesy of Michael and Sharon Reinheimer.* $150-165

House 'n Garden Ovenproof Serving-ware.
Serving set (using jam or mustard jars with covers, 531), slots in the lids for spoons, glazed in Mirror Brown trimmed in Ivory Foam. Overall height: 9" high. Jars, 4.25" high. *Courtesy of Thomas F. and Heather A. Evans.* $175-190

House 'n Garden Ovenproof Serving-ware.
Ball canister set in Mirror Brown trimmed in Ivory Foam. 9", 8", 7", and 6" in height. *Courtesy of Michael and Sharon Reinheimer.* $400-440

House 'n Garden Ovenproof Serving-ware.
Chip & dip set in Mirror Brown trimmed in Ivory Foam (not a normal production piece) with metal handle. 10.25 & 5.25" diameter *Courtesy of Lyle Applegate.* $75-85

House 'n Garden Ovenproof Serving-ware.
Ashtray glazed in Mirror Brown trimmed in Ivory Foam, A-5. *Courtesy of Thomas F. and Heather A. Evans.* $125-135

House 'n Garden Ovenproof Serving-ware Rainbow.
Soup mugs (14 oz.) and trays. Soup mugs, 5" diameter. Trays, 10" long.
Courtesy of the Collection of Betty and Joe Yonis. $35-40 sets

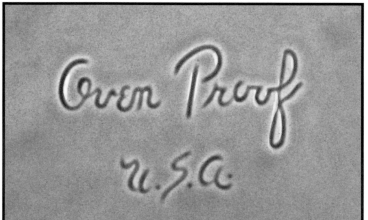

House 'n Garden
Ovenproof Serving-
ware Rainbow.
Individual leaf dishes
in Rainbow colors,
590, 7.25" in length.
*Courtesy of Michael
and Sharon
Reinheimer.* $15-20
each

House 'n Garden Ovenproof Serving-ware Rainbow. Leaf shape chip 'n dip in the Rainbow Tangerine glaze, 591, 12.25" long. *Courtesy of Michael and Sharon Reinheimer.* $25-30

Below:
House 'n Garden Ovenproof
Serving-ware Rainbow.
Rainbow Tangerine mixing bowls (largest with a pouring lip), French handled casseroles (with and without covers). Bowls: 8" & 7.25" diameter *Courtesy of Michael and Sharon Reinheimer.* Mixing bowls: 8", $25-30, 7.25", $20-25. Covered casserole, $20-25. Casserole, coverless, $15-16.

House 'n Garden Ovenproof Serving-ware Rainbow.
Rainbow Tangerine individual bean pot, covered butter dish, and ashtray. Ashtray, 8" diameter. *Courtesy of Michael and Sharon Reinheimer.* Left to right: $35-40; $20-25; $25-30

House 'n Garden Ovenproof Serving-ware Rainbow.
Rainbow Tangerine divided vegetable dish, cup and saucer, and creamer. *Courtesy of Michael and Sharon Reinheimer.* Left to right: $20-25; $15-16; $10-11

House 'n Garden Ovenproof Serving-ware Rainbow/ Miscellaneous.
Bud vase from the Rainbow line glazed in Tangerine with a Foam Edge, 9" high; bud vase (unidentified line) glazed in Moss Green with a Foam Edge. *Courtesy of Michael and Sharon Reinheimer.* Tangerine, $35-40; Moss Green, $20-25

House 'n Garden Ovenproof Serving-ware Rainbow.
Rainbow Green Agate bowls and oval divided serving dish, and oval casserole. Bowls, 8.5 and 5.25" diameter; oval serving dish, 11" and casserole, 10" long. *Courtesy of Michael and Sharon Reinheimer.* Bowls: 8.5", $15-16, 5.25", $10-11. Divided dish, $15-16. Casserole, $15-16.

House 'n Garden Ovenproof Serving-ware Rainbow. Rainbow Green Agate cookie jar, bean pot, and French handled casserole with cover. Cookie jar, 8" high. *Courtesy of Michael and Sharon Reinheimer.* $75-85; $35-40; $20-25

House 'n Garden Ovenproof Serving-ware Rainbow. Rainbow Green Agate teapot, creamer, cup and saucer, and mug. Teapot, 6.75" high. *Courtesy of Michael and Sharon Reinheimer.* $30-35; $10-11; $10-11; $15-16

House 'n Garden Ovenproof Serving-ware Rainbow. Rainbow Green Agate water jug (five pint), jug (two pint), and coffee pot, 11.5", 9" and 7" high jugs. *Courtesy of Michael and Sharon Reinheimer.* Jug (5 pt.), $20-25; jug (2 pt.), $15-16; coffee pot, $40-45

House 'n Garden Ovenproof Serving-ware Rainbow. Rainbow tidbit trays in Green Agate and Butterscotch. *Courtesy of Michael and Sharon Reinheimer.* Left to right: $50-55; $60-70

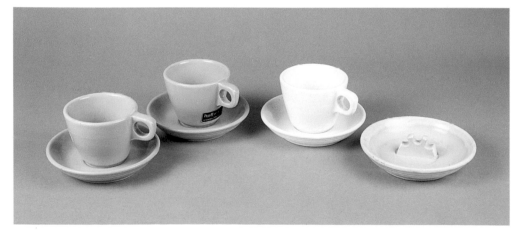

House 'n Garden Ovenproof Serving-ware Rainbow. The glaze colors of what would have become the next Rainbow line, had it ever been produced. Note the odd sample piece, an ashtray fashioned from a saucer. *Courtesy of the Collection of Betty and Joe Yonis.* Samples, $40-45 each

Adding to the diversity of the overall line were Provincial, Tangerine, Country Squire, Avocado, Almond and Mirror Almond. These
lines, featuring a variety of different glaze colorings and limited numbers of items taken from the overall House 'n Garden line, met with
varying success. Provincial was short lived, offered in 1961, featuring Mirror Brown exteriors with white interiors and lids. Over twenty
shapes were offered in Provincial.

House 'n Garden Ovenproof Serving-ware.
Provincial jug, 709, ice jug, 714, and sugar bowl (lid missing), 719. The jug measures 9" high.
All are marked only "Oven Proof USA." *Courtesy of Michael and Sharon Reinheimer.* Jug,
$40-45; ice jug, $40-45; sugar, $20-25

Above and left:
House 'n Garden Ovenproof
Serving-ware.
Provincial graduated mixing bowl
set, 8.5", 7", and 5.5" in diameter.
Provincial bowls have lips.
*Courtesy of Michael and Sharon
Reinheimer.* $30-35; $25-30;
$20-25. $75-90 set.

for the new way of life . . .

OVENPROOF **H**ouse 'n **G**arden Serving-ware

FOR YOUR DAILY NEEDS

| 669 | 600 Dinner Plate | 602 Mug | 603 Fruit | 601 Salad Plate |
| 6½" Soup/Salad | 10¼" Dia. | 9 oz. | 5¼" | 6½" |

604—4 PIECE PLACE SETTING

| 615 Salt Shaker | 616 Pepper Shaker | 618 | 619 Sugar Bowl | 627 Fr. Handled Casserole | 633 Fruit | 626 Beer Stein |
| w/cork 3¾" Hi. | w/cork 3¾" Hi. | Creamer 8 oz. | w/Cover 12 oz. | w/Cover 12 oz. | 6" | 16 oz. |

617 Salt & Pepper Set   620 Sugar & Creamer Set

| 622 Coffee Pot | 649 Tea Pot | 625 Jug | 621 Chip 'n Dip |
| w/Cover 8 Cup | w/Cover 5 Cup | 2 pt. | |

| 641 Oval Steak Plate | 642 Divided Vegetable Dish | 648 Deep Oval Casserole |
| 11¾" x 9" | 10¾" x 7¼" | w/Cover 2 qt. |

hull pottery company — crooksville, ohio *u.s.a.*

This page and following pages:
An advertisement and listings for the House 'n Garden Serving-ware in Avocado with ivory trim, dated November 1, 1969. Hull Pottery billed this ware as "the nation's number one line for casual living—the new and fashionable way of life." A 45 piece dinnerware set, 6-1095, was offered. *Courtesy of the Collection of Betty and Joe Yonis.*

666 Pie Plate	624 Ind. Bean Pot	610 Bean Pot	699 Luncheon Plate
9 1/4" Dia.	w/Cover 12 oz.	w/Cover 2 qt.	9 3/8" Dia.

698 Saucer	697 Cup	651 Jam or Mustard Jar w/Cover Set w/Spoon 12 oz.	661 Covered Butter Dish	674 Oval Bake 'n Serve Dish
5 7/8"	7 oz.		(1/4 lb. Capacity)	10" x 5" x 1 3/8"

624-4 Beer Stein 16 oz.
4 Piece Party Pack Set
(Individual Carton 6 Sets to Master)

604—Oven Proof 16 Piece Starter Set   **670—Oven Proof 16 Piece Starter Set**

4 - Fruits—5 1/4"	4 - Salad Plates—6 1/2"	4 - Fruits—6"	4 - Saucers—5 7/8"
4 - Mugs—9 oz.	4 - Dinner Plates—10 1/4" Dia.	4 - Cups—7 oz.	4 - Luncheon Plates—9 3/8" Dia.

House 'n Garden Serving-ware in AVOCADO, with ivory trim
OVENPROOF

"the nation's number one line
for casual living —
the new and fashionable way of life"

ITEM NO.	DESCRIPTION	PACKED	APPROX. WEIGHT	PRICE DOZEN
600	Dinner Plate 10-1/4"	1 doz.	24 lbs.	$ 6.96
601	Salad Plate 6-1/2"	2 doz.	18 lbs.	2.52
602	Mug 9 oz.	4 doz.	40 lbs.	3.36
602-4	Coffee Mug 9 oz. 4 Piece Party Pack Set (Individual carton—12 sets to master)	12 sets	40 lbs.	1.22 set
603	Fruit 5-1/4"	2 doz.	21 lbs.	2.52
604	Starter Set consisting of: 4 only 600 Dinner Plates 10-1/4" 4 only 601 Salad Plates 6-1/2" 4 only 602 Mugs 9 oz. 4 only 603 Fruits 5-1/4"	1 set	17 lbs.	4.83 set
610	Bean Pot w/cover 2 qt.	1/2 doz.	21 lbs.	12.60
613	French Handled Casserole 12 oz.	2 doz.	21 lbs.	3.36
615	Salt Shaker w/cork 3-3/4" Hi.	2 doz.	15 lbs.	3.72
616	Pepper Shaker w/cork 3-3/4" Hi.	2 doz.	15 lbs.	3.72
617	Salt & Pepper Set	12 sets	15 lbs.	.63 set
618	Creamer 8 oz.	2 doz.	18 lbs.	3.24
619	Sugar Bowl w/cover 12 oz.	2 doz.	21 lbs.	4.56
620	Sugar & Creamer Set	12 sets	20 lbs.	.65 set
621	Chip 'n Dip	1/3 doz.	13 lbs.	20.16
622	Coffee Pot w/cover 8 cup	1/2 doz.	20 lbs.	20.16
624	Individual Bean Pot w/cover 12 oz.	2 doz.	21 lbs.	4.56
625	Jug 2 pt.	1 doz.	21 lbs.	6.96
626	Beer Stein 16 oz.	2 doz.	28 lbs.	4.80
626-4	Beer Stein 16 oz. 4 Piece Party Pack Set (Individual carton—6 sets to master)	6 sets	30 lbs.	1.79 set
627	French Handled Casserole w/cover	2 doz.	33 lbs.	4.32
633	Fruit 6"	2 doz.	21 lbs.	3.12
641	Oval Steak Plate 11-3/4" x 9"	1 doz.	27 lbs.	7.56
642	Divided Vegetable Dish 10-3/4" x 7-1/4"	1/2 doz.	15 lbs.	10.08
648	Deep Oval Casserole w/cover 2 qt.	1/3 doz.	17 lbs.	15.96
649	Tea Pot w/cover 5 cup	1/2 doz.	14 lbs.	10.08
650	Jam or Mustard Jar w/cover 12 oz.	2 doz.	21 lbs.	4.56
651	Jam or Mustard Jar w/cover set consisting of: 1 only 650—Jam or Mustard Jar w/cover 1 only 652—Crystal Plastic Spoon	24 sets	21 lbs.	.48 set
652	Jam or Mustard Spoon/Crystal Plastic	2 doz.	1/2 lbs.	1.47
661	Covered Butter Dish (1/4 lb. capacity)	1 doz.	18 lbs.	7.32
666	Pie Plate 9-1/4" dia.	1 doz.	24 lbs.	6.96
669	Soup or Salad Bowl 6-1/2"	2 doz.	29 lbs.	4.56

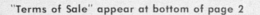

"Terms of Sale" appear at bottom of page 2

House'n Garden Serving-ware continued

ITEM NO.	DESCRIPTION	PACKED	APPROX. WEIGHT	PRICE DOZEN
670	Starter Set consisting of: .... 4 only 633 Fruits 6" 4 only 697 Cups 7 oz. 4 only 698 Saucers 5-7/8" 4 only 699 Plates 9-3/8"	1 set	15 lbs.	$ 4.73 set
674	Oval Bake 'n Serve Dish 10" x 5" x 1-3/8"	2 doz.	28 lbs.	6.96
697	Cup 7 oz.	4 doz.	27 lbs.	3.24
698	Saucer 5-7/8"	2 doz.	14 lbs.	2.52
699	Luncheon Plate 9-3/8"	1 doz.	19 lbs.	6.12
6-1095	45 Piece Dinner Set consisting of: .... 8 only 600 Dinner Plate 10-1/4" 8 only 601 Salad Plate 6-1/2" 8 only 603 Fruit 5-1/4" 8 only 697 Cup 7 oz. 8 only 698 Saucer 5-7/8" 1 only 620 Sugar & Creamer Set 1 only 641 Steak Plate 11-3/4" x 9" 1 only 642 Divided Vegetable Dish 10-3/4" x 7-1/4"	1 set	43 lbs.	13.76 set

Sold only in standard packages—no extra packing charge • Terms: 1% 15 days net 30—fob Crooksville, Ohio
NO ALLOWANCE FOR BREAKAGE—CLAIMS MUST BE FILED WITH COMMON CARRIER
THE COMPLETE HOUSE 'N GARDEN LINE (60 shapes) IN "MIRROR BROWN" IS CATALOGUED AS 500 SERIES.
Items listed in both Mirror Brown and Avocado may be assorted in cartons at no extra cost.

OVEN-PROOF

HULL POTTERY · CROOKSVILLE, OHIO

604 – 16 pc. Set

Pottery

- **4 DINNER PLATES**
- **4 SALAD PLATES**
- **4 FRUITS**
- **4 MUGS**

An ad for the House 'n Garden 16 piece set in Avocado. *Courtesy of the Collection of Betty and Joe Yonis.*

House 'n Garden Ovenproof Serving-ware Avocado.
Oval steak platter, 641, dinner plate, 600, salad plate, 601, salt & pepper shakers, 615 & 616, bean pot with cover, 610, fruit bowl, 603, and oval bake 'n serve dish, 674. The platter measures 11.75" x 9". *Courtesy of the Collection of Betty and Joe Yonis.* Platter: $40-50; dinner plate, $11-12; salad plate, $6-7; shakers, $60-70; bean pot, $35-40; fruit bowl, $6-7; bake 'n serve, $16-17

House 'n Garden Ovenproof Serving-ware Avocado.
Teapot with cover, 649, sugar bowl with cover, 619, 8 oz. creamer, 618, and cup, 697, and saucer, 698. Teapot 6.5" high. *Courtesy of the Collection of Betty and Joe Yonis.* Teapot, $35-40; sugar, $10-11; creamer, $10-11; cup & saucer, $15-16

House 'n Garden Ovenproof
Serving-ware.
Circular trays glazed in Mirror
Brown trimmed in Ivory Foam &
Almond. 11" diameter. *Courtesy of
Thomas F. and Heather A. Evans;
courtesy of Michael and Sharon
Reinheimer.* Mirror Brown tray,
$125-150; Almond tray, $125-150

House 'n Garden Ovenproof
Serving-ware.
Mirror Almond oval serving dish,
serving tray, snack tray with open
French handled casserole, salad
plate, and ramekin. Plate, 6.75"
diameter. *Courtesy of Michael and
Sharon Reinheimer.* Dish, $25-30;
serving tray, $50-55; snack tray with
casserole, $30-35; plate, $10-11;
ramekin, $25-30

House 'n Garden
Ovenproof Serving-
ware.
Mirror Almond mixing
bowl, soup or salad
bowl, fruit bowl, 7",
6.5" and 5.25"
diameter. *Courtesy of
Michael and Sharon
Reinheimer.* Left to
right: $20-25; $10-11;
$10-11

Tangerine was offered exclusively through J.C. Penney from 1963-1967. Tangerine is also known as either Burnt Orange or Golden Anniversary. Around forty shapes filled out the Tangerine House 'n Garden casual Serving-ware line. Country Squire featured the Green Agate color from Rainbow, trimmed with Turquoise. Once again, around forty items were offered in the Country Squire House 'n Garden line.

Hull Pottery experimented in 1965 with a House 'n Garden Swirl line. The wares were decorated with a swirling pattern in the molded design. Of this experiment, plates, bowls in two sizes, cups and saucers, a stein and a French-handled casserole remain.

House 'n Garden Ovenproof Serving-ware.
Experimental Swirl dinner-ware. Plate, 10" diameter; stein, 5" high. *Courtesy of Michael and Sharon Reinheimer.* Plate, $50-75; stein, $65-75

Avocado was introduced to the House 'n Garden Serving-ware ranks in 1968 and remained in production through 1971. Avocado came with an Ivory foam edge at times. Thirty pieces were included in this line.

Continuing to experiment with the line, Hull produced a Bicentennial line glazed in Mirror Brown or Satin Avo-

cado. Molded eagles and stars adorned the wares. Included among the pieces were a large pitcher, a sugar and creamer, mugs and steins, bean pots and low casseroles. These patriotic expressions were produced in 1975/1976.

House 'n Garden Ovenproof Serving-ware Bicentennial.
Pitcher, cream & sugar, mug, salt & pepper. Pitcher 7.5" high. *Courtesy of the Collection of Betty and Joe Yonis.* Pitcher, $200-220; cream & sugar, $100-110 set; mug, $90-100; salt & pepper, $200-220 set.

House 'n Garden Ovenproof Serving-ware Bicentennial. Salt and pepper shakers, 3" high. *Courtesy of Thomas F. and Heather A. Evans.* $80-90

House 'n Garden Ovenproof Serving-ware Bicentennial. Covered bean, covered casserole, and two bowls. Bean, 8" high. *Courtesy of the Collection of Betty and Joe Yonis.* Bean, $150-165; casserole, $140-155; bowls, $125-135 each

Late-comers to the House 'n Garden line were Almond and Mirror Almond, produced from 1981 to 1983. Both were offered with a Caramel foam edge, although many of the accessory items in Almond did not receive this edge trimming. Around thirty items were offered.

Very popular among collectors of the House 'n Garden line are the chicken and duck casseroles. The lids are molded in the form of ... a chicken or a duck, as one might expect.

Serving-ware
Crestone

The Crestone ovenproof casual Serving-ware line was produced from 1965 to 1967. Roughly thirty-five pieces were made for the line. These were decorated in a new high gloss turquoise glaze with white foam edge trim. A striking two cup coffee carafe was part of the line, accompanied by a 7 oz. stacking coffee cup into which the carafe would nestle.

Crestone.
Dinner plate, 300, 10" diameter; teapot, 349, 6.25" high; sugar bowl with cover, 319, 8 oz.; creamer, 318, 8 oz.; coffee mug, 302, 9 oz., and gravy boat or syrup, 310, 10 oz. (a saucer was offered for the gravy boat/syrup, 311, 6.5" diameter). Note the similarity in body form between the Crestone dinner plate and the Avocado luncheon plate, 331, 9.5" diameter. *Courtesy of the Collection of Betty and Joe Yonis.* Plates, $10-11 & $7-8. Teapot, $40-45. Cream and sugar, $25-30 each. Mug, $2-3. Gravy boat or syrup, part of a $40-45 set (with saucer).

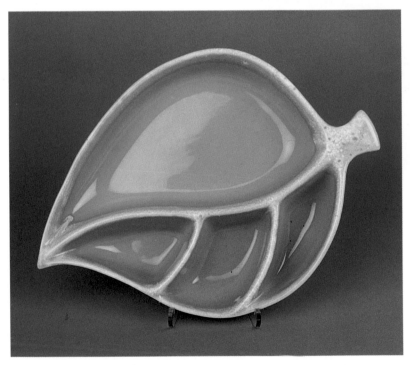

Crestone
Chip 'n dip leaf, 321, 14.5" long. *Courtesy of Michael and Sharon Reinheimer.* $50-55

Crestone, etc.
Left to right: House 'n Garden Ovenproof Serving-ware Mirror Brown and Crestone coffee carafes, 7" high each. *Courtesy of the Collection of Betty and Joe Yonis.* $50-55 each complete

Gingerbread Man

In 1978, a fanciful gingerbread man server was introduced. In 1982, the gingerbread man appeared in the
form of a large cookie jar, with his cheerful face also appearing on a child's bowl and a mug. A gingerbread man
combination coaster and spoon rest was also produced.
A Gingerbread Express did not get the chance to leave
the station as the company closed before this imaginative canister set was beyond the trial stage. As test pieces,
the Express sets produced did not bear any Hull
manufacturer's mark. The train station itself, along with a
candy jar, were never put into mass-production. Most of
the Gingerbread Man line was glazed in Mirror Brown,
although the tan (tawny) and gray (flint) glazes used in
the Ridge line were added in time.

It is interesting to note that as the company drew to a
close, labor unrest forced Hull to subcontract with West-
ern Stoneware of Illinois for the production of many of
the Gingerbread Man cookie jars.

Gingerbread Man.
Cookie jars in three glazes. Sand, 223; Brown, 323; Gray, 123. 11.25" high. *Courtesy of Michael and Sharon Reinheimer.* Sand, $500-550; brown, $200-220; gray, $450-495

Above and right:
Gingerbread Express.
Canister set, with engine, coal car, passenger & caboose. *Courtesy of Thomas F. and Heather A. Evans.* $5000-6000; $1250-1500 each piece

Gingerbread Express.
Unique hand painted version of the Ginger-
bread Express. *Courtesy of the Collection of
Betty and Joe Yonis.* $6000-7000

Gingerbread Man.
Gingerbread Junction Depot cookie jar (goes with the train) & Gingerbread Man mug,
324, and bowl, 325. 12" high cookie jar. *Courtesy of Michael and Sharon Reinheimer.*
Depot, $275-300; mug, $125-135; bowl, $125-135

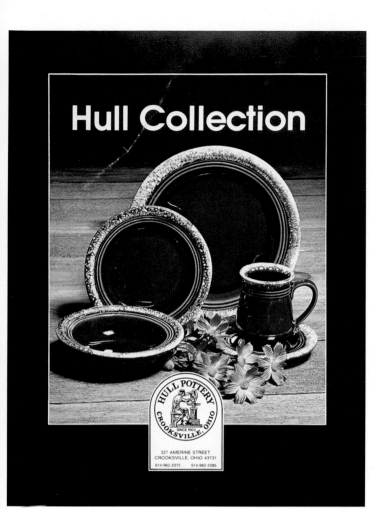

This page:
Advertisement for Hull Collection wares with Mirror Brown glazing and a distinctive ring edge design. *Courtesy of the Collection of Betty and Joe Yonis.*

5439 — Consists of 1 each: 5436, 5438, 5440

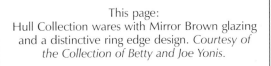

This page:
Hull Collection wares with Mirror Brown glazing
and a distinctive ring edge design. *Courtesy of
the Collection of Betty and Joe Yonis.*

504 16 Pc. Starter - Consists of 1 each: 500, 501, 302, 503

Hull Collection.
Mirror Brown "Ring Ware" (a short lived line)
trimmed in Ivory Foam: plates & bowls. Plates, 10",
8.5", 7.25" diameters. Bowls, 8" & 7" diameters.
Courtesy of Thomas F. and Heather A. Evans. Plate,
10" dinner, $25-30; plate, 8.5" luncheon, $20-25;
plate, 7.25" salad, $15-16; bowl, 20 oz. soup, $30-
35; bowl, 12 oz soup, $20-25

Hull Collection.
Mirror Brown Ring Ware trimmed in Ivory
Foam: platter, serving dish, and covered
casserole. Platter, 12" long. Serving dish,
11" long. *Courtesy of Thomas F. and
Heather A. Evans.* Platter, $40-45; serving
dish, $45-50; casserole, $75-85

Hull Collection.
Mirror Brown Ring Ware trimmed in
Ivory Foam: stemmed coffee pot,
creamer & sugar, cup & saucer, and
pedestal mug. Coffee pot, 8.25" high.
*Courtesy of Thomas F. and Heather A.
Evans.* Coffee pot, $75-85; cream, $35-
40; sugar, $40-45; coffee cup, $25-30;
saucer, $10-11; mug, $35-40

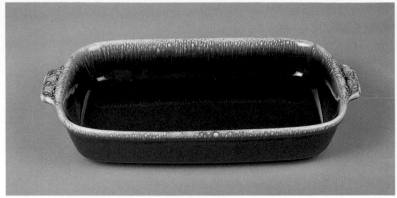

Hull Collection.
Mirror Brown Ring Ware trimmed in Ivory Foam: gravy boat and undertray, custard cup, salt, pepper, and cheese shakers. Gravy, 3.5" high; undertray, 6.5" diameter; shakers, 6.25" high. *Courtesy of Thomas F. and Heather A. Evans.* Gravy, $45-50; undertray, $10-11; custard, $35-40; salt & pepper, $80-90; cheese, $50-55

Hull Collection.
Mirror Brown Ring Ware trimmed in Ivory Foam: 2 qt. baker, 567, 14" across tab handles. *Courtesy of Thomas F. and Heather A. Evans.* $110-120

Hull Collection.
Mirror Brown Ring Ware trimmed in Ivory Foam: mixing bowls, 10, 8, 6" diameters. *Courtesy of Thomas F. and Heather A. Evans.* $95-110 set: 10", $45-50; 8", $30-35; 6", $20-25

Hull Collection.
Mirror Brown Ring Ware trimmed in Ivory Foam: canister set ranging in size from 9.5" to 7.25" high. *Courtesy of Thomas F. and Heather A. Evans.* $700-770

Hull Collection.
Mirror Brown Ring Ware trimmed in
Ivory Foam: cookie jar and bean pot,
9.5" high and 8.5" high respectively.
*Courtesy of Thomas F. and Heather A.
Evans.* Cookie jar, $125-135; bean pot,
$125-135

Hull Collection.
Mirror Brown Ring Ware trimmed in Ivory Foam:
pitcher, 7" high to lip. *Courtesy of Thomas F. and
Heather A. Evans.* $65-75

Hull Collection.
Mirror Brown Ring Ware trimmed
in Ivory Foam: ewer and basin,
8.5" high ewer, 12" diameter
basin. *Courtesy of Thomas F. and
Heather A. Evans.* $120-130

Hull Collection.
Mushroom salt and pepper
shakers offered with the Hull
Collection Ring Ware line. Rougly
4" high each. *Courtesy of the
Collection of Betty and Joe Yonis.*
$20-25 set

Food for thought.

Hull's Garden Dishes grace table settings two ways, not only as functional planters but also as attractive garnish and snack bowls. That's an appetizing thought for your customers!

† F77 Fancy Oval Garden Dish
11½" × 5¾" × 3"

† A6 Scroll Flower Dish
9" × 5½" × 3¼"

† F41 Rect. Low Flower Bowl
7½" × 5⅝" × 2¾"

* F61 Heart-Shaped Garden Dish
7" × 3" High

† Best-Selling Carry-Over Items
* New Items

(Knives and flowers not included)

Hull Pottery Company's "Hull Collection" wares in Ridge collection colors of grey, sand, and brown. *Courtesy of the Collection of Betty and Joe Yonis.*

12 OZ. CONTINENTAL MUG
GRAY
2571 SAND
571 BROWN

21 OZ. SOUP OR SALAD BOWL
1569 GRAY
2569 SAND
569 BROWN

50 OZ. SQUARE BAKER
1568 GRAY
2568 SAND
568 BROWN

PIE PLATE, 9¼"
1566 GRAY
2566 SAND
566 BROWN

34 OZ. INDIVIDUAL OVAL SPAGHETTI PLATE
1581 GRAY
2581 SAND
581 BROWN

OVAL WELL 'N TREE STEAK PLATE
593 BROWN

9 OZ. FRENCH HANDLED CASSEROLE W/COVER
579 BROWN

OZ. FRENCH HANDLED CASSEROLE
562 BROWN

16 OZ. OVAL SERVING DISH
1574 GRAY
2574 SAND
574 BROWN

9½ OZ. SMALL OVAL SERVING DISH
1573 GRAY
2573 SAND
573 BROWN

BAKE & SERVE, 6½"
1589 GRAY
2589 SAND
589 BROWN

8 OZ. CUSTARD CUP
176 GRAY
276 SAND
376 BROWN

MUSHROOM SALT & PEPPER SET
587/588 BROWN

2½ OZ. RAMEKIN
1600 GRAY
2600 SAND
600 BROWN

4 PC. CANISTER SET
160 GRAY
260 SAND
360 BROWN

GINGERBREAD MAN COOKIE JAR
123 GRAY
223 SAND
323 BROWN

38 OZ. CASSEROLE W/DUCK COVER
15280 GRAY
25280 SAND
5280 BROWN

68 OZ. CASSEROLE W/CHICKEN COVER
15850 GRAY
25850 SAND
5850 BROWN

SITTING PIGGY BANK
1196 GRAY
2196 SAND
196 BROWN

32 OZ. CASSEROLE W/COVER
114 GRAY
214 SAND
314 BROWN

CORKY PIGGY BANK
1195 GRAY
2195 SAND
195 BROWN

18 OZ. SERVER W/HANDLE
1595 GRAY
2595 SAND
595 BROWN

13 OZ. GARLIC CELLAR
1505 GRAY
2505 SAND
3505 BROWN

GINGERBREAD BOY COASTER/SPOON REST, 5" x 5"
199 GRAY
299 SAND
399 BROWN

GINGERBREAD MAN SERVER, 10" x 10"
1198 GRAY
2198 SAND
198 BROWN

Hull Pottery Company's "Hull Collection" wares in Ridge collection colors of grey, sand, and brown. *Courtesy of the Collection of Betty and Joe Yonis.*

Hull "Collection" Ridge. Flint Ridge platter, plates, 12 oz. Continental mug (the pedestaled mug), cup and saucer, bowl, and salt & pepper shakers. Platter 12" long. Plates 10 & 7" diameter *Courtesy of the Collection of Betty and Joe Yonis*. Platter, $35-40; plates, $12-13 & $8-9; mug, $11-12; cup & saucer, $25-30; bowl, $6-7; salt & pepper shakers, $60-70

Hull "Collection" Ridge. Possibly Flint Ridge servers/flower bowls, 8" & 6.5" long. *Courtesy of the Collection of Betty and Joe Yonis*. $45-50; $40-45

Hull "Collection" Ridge. Tawny Ridge Platter, salad plate, 12 oz. Continental mug, creamer, 13 oz. garlic cellar, cup and saucer, and mug. Platter, 12" long; salad plate, 6.5" diameter. *Courtesy of the Collection of Betty and Joe Yonis*. Platter, $35-40; plate, $8-9; Continental mug, $11-12; creamer, $11-12; garlic cellar, $16-17; cup & saucer, $25-30; mug, $6-7

Hull "Collection" Ridge.
Walnut Ridge Platter, dinner plate, salad plate, cup and saucer, bowl, and salt and pepper shaker. Platter, 12" long; dinner plate, 10" diameter; salad plate, 6.5" diameter. *Courtesy of Thomas F. and Heather A. Evans.* Platter, $35-40; dinner plate, $12-13; salad plate, $8-9; cup & saucer, $25-30; salt & pepper shakers, $65-75

Hull "Collection" Ridge.
Walnut Ridge rectangular snack tray, mug, covered 32 oz. casserole, custard cup, cream & covered sugar. Snack tray, 9.5" long. *Courtesy of Thomas F and Heather A. Evans.* Tray, $35-40; mug, $8-9; casserole, $30-35; custard, $15-16; cream, $35-40; sugar, $30-35

Hull "Collection" in Ridge Colors.
Corky Piggy Bank in brown, 195. *Courtesy of the Collection of Betty and Joe Yonis.* $100-110

Hull "Collection" Ridge.
Walnut Ridge canister set, ranging in height from 8.5" to 6". *Courtesy of Thomas F. and Heather A. Evans.* $600-660

Hull "Collection" in Ridge Colors.
Corky Piggy Banks in sand, 2195 and 2196, and gray, 1195 and 1196. *Courtesy of Michael and Sharon Reinheimer.* Sitting, $375-410; standing, $350-385

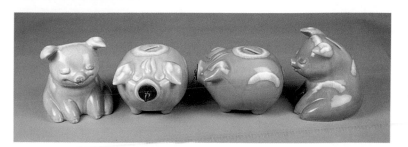

436 6" Bowl

Heartland.
Platter, plates, and bowl.
Courtesy of the Collection of Betty and Joe Yonis. Platter, 12", $25-30; plate,10", $12-13; plate, 8.75", $15-16; plates, 7.25", $8-9; bowl, 7" diameter, $12-13.

Heartland.
Pie, 466, and quiche, 444, dishes, 11" & 10" diameter respectively. *Courtesy of the Collection of Betty and Joe Yonis.* $60-65 & $125-135.

Heartland.
This appears to be a paint tumbler on the left decorated in the Heartland motif and a Heartland custard cup. *Courtesy of the Collection of Betty and Joe Yonis.* Tumbler, 3.5" high, $20-25. Custard, 2.5" high, $35-40.

Heartland.
Salt and pepper shakers, covered sugar and creamer, gravy boat (without undertray), and two mugs, with and without pedestal. Salt shaker, 6.25" high. *Courtesy of the Collection of Betty and Joe Yonis.* Salt & Pepper shakers, $40-45 each. Sugar & creamer, $40-45 each. Gravy boat, $75-85. Mugs, $25-30 each.

Heartland.
Pitcher and bowl set. Pitcher, 8.5" high. Bowl, 12" diameter *Courtesy of the Collection of Betty and Joe Yonis.* $120-135 set.

Heartland.
Flour, sugar, coffee and tea canisters. Flour, 9.5" high. *Courtesy of the Collection of Betty and Joe Yonis.* $300-350 set.

Heartland.
Two quart baker, 14" across handles. *Courtesy of Thomas F. and Heather A. Evans.* $50-55

Heartland.
Mixing bowls, tab handled baker, and serving tray with handle. Mixing bowls, 439 3 piece set, 10", 8" & 6" diameters; tab handled baker, 467, 9.5" across tabs; serving tray, 495, 11.5" with handle. *Courtesy of the Collection of Betty and Joe Yonis.* Mixing bowls, $100-110 set. Tab handled baker, $40-45. Serving tray, $50-55.

Heartland.
Covered bakers, chicken and duck. Duck, 4280, 10" long x 7.5" high. Chicken, 4850, 10" long x 9.5" high. *Courtesy of the Collection of Betty and Joe Yonis.* $150-165 each.

Country (Blue) Belle.
Platter and salt and pepper shakers. Platter, 12" long. *Courtesy of the Collection of Betty and Joe Yonis.* Platter: $25-30; shakers, $100-110 set

Recently produced Hull Pottery advertising plaques. The left plaque with gold lettering is unique. 5" wide x 4" high. *Courtesy of the Collection of Betty and Joe Yonis.* Left to right: $250-275; $75-85

Hull Pottery Association

Since 1995, the Hull Pottery Association has been offering commemoratives to its members. We'll end our modest survey of Hull Pottery wares with these nostalgic modern tributes to this much-loved pottery.

Hull Commemoratives produced in 1995, 1996, and 1997 for the Hull Pottery Association. *Courtesy of the Collection of Betty and Joe Yonis.* Left to right: $500-550; $400-440; $400-440

Hull Commemoratives for 1998 and 1999. *Courtesy of the Collection of Betty and Joe Yonis.* Left to right: $200-220; $250-275

Bibliography

Bassett, Mark. *Introducing Roseville Pottery*. Atglen, Pennsylvania: Schiffer Publishing, 1999.

Cushion, J.P. and W.B. Honey. *Handbook of Pottery & Porcelain Marks*. London: Faber and Faber, 1980.

Gick-Burke, Barbara Loveless. *Collector's Guide to Hull Pottery. The Dinnerware Lines*. Paducah, Kentucky: Collector Books, 1993.

Hull, Joan Gray. *Hull. The Heavenly Pottery*. Huron, South Dakota: Creative Printing, 1999 (6th Edition).

Konyah, Dee. "History." In Hull, Joan Gray. *Hull. The Heavenly Pottery*. Huron, South Dakota: Creative Printing, 1999 (6th Edition).

Roberts, Brenda. *The Collector's Encyclopedia of Hull Pottery*. Paducah, Kentucky: Collector Books, 1980.

_____. *Roberts' Ultimate Encyclopedia of Hull Pottery*. Marceline, Missouri: Walsworth Publishing Company, 1992.

Schneider, Mike. *The Complete Cookie Jar Book*. West Chester, Pennsylvania: Schiffer Publishing, 1991.

Snyder, Jeffrey B. *Depression Pottery*. Atglen, Pennsylvania: Schiffer Publishing, 1999.

_____. *McCoy Pottery*. Atglen, Pennsylvania: Schiffer Publishing, 1999a.

_____. *A Pocket Guide to Flow Blue*. Atglen, Pennsylvania: Schiffer Publishing, 1995.

Index